IMAGES OF WAR

UNITED STATES MARINE CORPS IN THE KOREAN WAR

RARE PHOTOGRAPHS FROM WARTIME ARCHIVES

Michael Green

Pen & Sword
MILITARY

First published in Great Britain in 2021 by
PEN & SWORD MILITARY
an imprint of
Pen & Sword Books Ltd
47 Church Street
Barnsley
South Yorkshire
S70 2AS

Copyright © Michael Green, 2021

ISBN 978-1-52676-537-6

Typeset by Concept, Huddersfield, West Yorkshire HD4 5JL.
Printed and bound in India by Replika Press Pvt. Ltd.

Pen & Sword Books Limited incorporates the imprints of Atlas, Archaeology, Aviation, Discovery, Family History, Fiction, History, Maritime, Military, Military Classics, Politics, Select, Transport, True Crime, Air World, Frontline Publishing, Leo Cooper, Remember When, Seaforth Publishing, The Praetorian Press, Wharncliffe Local History, Wharncliffe Transport, Wharncliffe True Crime and White Owl.

For a complete list of Pen & Sword titles please contact
PEN & SWORD BOOKS LIMITED
47 Church Street, Barnsley, South Yorkshire S70 2AS, England
E-mail: enquiries@pen-and-sword.co.uk
Website: www.pen-and-sword.co.uk

Contents

Dedication

This dedication goes to Marine Private First Class Eugene A. Obregon. He was posthumously awarded the Medal of Honor for an action that took place during the fighting for the South Korean capital city of Seoul on 26 September 1950. His citation reads as follows:

> While serving as an ammunition carrier of a machine gun squad in a Marine Rifle Company which was temporarily pinned down by hostile fire, Private First Class Obregon observed a fellow Marine fall wounded in the line of fire. Armed only with a pistol, he unhesitatingly dashed from his covered position to the side of the casualty. Firing his pistol with one hand as he ran, he grasped his comrade by the arm with his other hand and, despite the great peril to himself, dragged him to the side of the road. Still, under enemy fire, he was bandaging the man's wounds when hostile troops of approximately platoon strength began advancing toward his position. Quickly seizing the wounded Marine's carbine, he placed his own body as a shield in front of him and lay there firing accurately and effectively into the hostile group until he himself was fatally wounded by enemy machine-gun fire.

Foreword

When the Korean War – the 'Forgotten War' – began, it raised three major issues that continue to impact us today, for better or worse. The first was that the United Nations (UN) authorized the use of force against member nations to stop an invasion. When the war began, it was the first time since the UN began after the Second World War that the Security Council authorized the use of force to repel an invading army.

Secondly, the Korean War would be the first time that the US military would fight under a different flag, not the Stars and Stripes. Although under the auspices of the UN, there was no doubt that although under a different flag, American forces, military leadership and political will would come from the United States.

Finally, and most importantly, the Korean War saved the United States Marine Corps from extinction. There was a growing movement within and outside of government to take the fiercest and most determined fighters during the Second World War, the iconic 'raggedy ass Marines' and demobilize them except for ceremonial units like the Marine Corps Band. It would take the Korean War to halt this demobilization of the Marines.

Following the Second World War, the United States was war-weary. There was massive demobilization of the services, from more than 12 million in uniform at the end of 1945 to slightly over 1 million poorly-trained, equipped and led troops by June 1950. The Marines, for example, were down to two sparsely-filled divisions. President Harry S. Truman, Congress and the Secretary of Defense Louis Johnson wanted what we would call today a 'peace dividend' by massive demobilization and the selling of equipment through foreign military aid.

Additionally, Johnson slashed military budgets to 'bare bones' existence, went on a personal warpath to challenge military leadership in the hopes of relieving many senior officers, and combined the Army, Navy and Air Force into one military organization. Even the Chief of Naval Operations dismissed the Marines. Johnson and Truman had a hard time in justifying the Navy having their own police force in the Marines, as the Navy and Marine Corps aviation took assets and budgets from the Air Force and performed the same mission. Even Dwight D. Eisenhower as Chief of Staff of the Army saw the Marines as duplicating the Army mission and wanted the Marines stripped of combat units and reduced to ceremonial responsibilities.

With this as a background, Michael Green's latest work, *United States Marine Corps in the Korean War*, brings forth a compelling overview of the war, complete with archival photos and sourced from official military histories. Through his narrative, Green shows exactly why the Marines were needed as part of a combined arms force that exemplified valour, courage and tenacity; first as a fire brigade to save a deteriorating perimeter, then as the main element for an amphibious assault at Inchon through the harrowing days of the Chosin Reservoir through to the armistice.

After Korea, the Marines would again prove their worth in the jungles of Vietnam, the deserts of the Middle East and in the mountains and villages of Afghanistan. Every military force, regardless of where they are from, can never think about going into battle without the 'raggedy ass Marines' on their side. *Semper Fidelis*.

Randy R. Talbot
US Army Command Historian (retired)

Acknowledgements

All the historical images in this work, with a few exceptions, come, from the National Archives (NA) or the Marine Corps Historical Center collection (USMC). Individuals who supplied images receive credit in the captions.

Note to the Reader

Due to the book's format and size, this work is only a very broad overview of the Marine Corps' involvement in the Korean War. The Marine Corps Historical Center has released, over the years, a great many well-researched publications detailing the ins and outs of the Korean conflict. These publications can be acquired in print or downloaded from the internet for those who wish to continue researching the subject matter.

Chapter One

The Opening Moves

On Sunday morning, 25 June 1950, approximately 90,000 soldiers of the North Korean People's Army (NKP or NKPA) poured into South Korea. Leading their assault were 150 T-34-85 medium tanks supplied by the Soviet Union. They had provided the NKPA with a total of 285 of the medium tanks. The Soviet Union had also outfitted the North Koreans with everything from submachine guns to heavy artillery and trained the troops in how to employ them.

All the North Korean invasion plans of South Korea were drawn up by Soviet Army generals who had the wartime experience that the generals of the NKPA lacked. Joseph Stalin told Kim Il-sung, premier/dictator of the Democratic People's Republic of Korea (DPRK), that the Soviet Union would not come to his aid if the invasion failed. Stalin suggested that Kim Il-sung seek the assistance of the People's Republic of China (PRC), known to Americans as Red China, which had established itself in 1949.

The PRC's leadership was aware of North Korea's planned invasion and had offered military assistance if the United States intervened. Nonetheless, Kim Il-sung rejected the offer. Confident of a quick victory and that the United States would not intervene, he also believed that the South Korean civilian population would rise against their American-supported government once the invasion began.

The Other Side

The Republic of Korea Army (ROK or ROKA), formed in November 1948, had approximately 100,000 men divided among eight infantry divisions. Four of the newly-raised ROK divisions had positions along the '38th Parallel' (referring to a northern longitude line), the designated border between North and South Korea.

By the end of June 1948, the last US occupation troops were gone from South Korea, leaving only the 500-member Korean Military Assistance Group to train the ROKA. The US Army did see fit to leave behind arms and equipment for 50,000 men. The American government, however, had not seen fit to provide any medium or heavy artillery or tanks to the newly-formed ROKA.

The lack of more extensive American military aid was deliberate. The American government feared that Syngman Rhee, South Korea's president and dictator, would

> **The Dividing Line**
>
> The 38th Parallel was an artificial border line drawn by the United States War Department (the forerunner of the Department of Defense) at the end of the Second World War. The intention was to temporarily divide Korea into two areas of control in which the surrender of Japanese military units still in-country would be accepted. The Soviet Union was assigned Northern Korea and the United States Southern Korea.

take it upon himself to invade North Korea had he a more credible military force and embroil the United States in the resulting conflict.

When the North Korean invasion began, reliable information proved unavailable. Senior American leadership first thought it was a limited incursion, as had happened before, and that the ROKA would be able to repel it. That belief came from the US Military Advisory Group to the Republic of Korea (KMAG) established on 1 July 1949. Its commanding officer had confidence in the ROKA and dismissed the NKPA.

Surprise, Surprise

The North Korean invasion often is portrayed as a complete surprise to the United States government and its military. However, this was not the case. As early as 1949, American intelligence services inside and outside South Korea had picked up ominous signs that a North Korean invasion was a strong possibility.

US Army advisors in South Korea and the ROKA senior leadership also knew in the weeks before the North Korean invasion that something was afoot. General Douglas MacArthur, the commanding officer of General Headquarters, Far East Command (GHQ FECOM) and his chief of staff Major General (MG) Charles A. Willoughby did not take heed of any of the numerous warnings.

Time to Act

Once it became clear that the North Koreans had invaded South Korea and that the ROKA had no chance of stopping the NKPA, President Truman committed American airpower on 28 June 1950. That airpower included US Navy and US Marine Corps squadrons flying from aircraft carriers of the Seventh Fleet, operating from Japan.

On 30 June President Truman authorized the commitment of American ground forces to the conflict. The senior leadership of the American government and military believed at the time that the North Korean invasion might be the opening act for a possible Soviet-directed worldwide Communist offensive.

On 27 June the UN had called for other countries to aid the United States in repelling the NKPA invasion of South Korea. Truman's military commitment to

South Korea was, therefore, to take place under the auspices of the UN. General MacArthur would be appointed as commander of all UN forces and consequently received an additional title as Commander-in-Chief, Far East (CINCFE) on 24 July while still retaining oversight of GHQ FECOM.

American Ground Involvement

At the time of the North Korean invasion the only US Army ground combat units in the region were on occupation duty in Japan. These consisted of four under-strength US Army infantry divisions, the 1st Cavalry (an honorary title) 7th, 24th and 25th divisions, and the US Army 29th Regimental Combat Team (RCT).

The four US Army divisions in Japan and the RCT belonged to the 'Eighth US Army' commanded by Lieutenant General (LTG) Walton H. Walker. The abbreviation for the Eighth US Army was 'EUSA'. On 17 July the EUSA assumed oversight of the ROKA.

Within the US Army command structure field armies, such as the EUSA, served as administrative organizations which directed from one to four corps. Corps, in turn, oversaw from one to five divisions. Eight US Army divisions eventually served during the Korean War, under the oversight of three US Army corps: the I, IX and X.

The first US Army ground combat unit rushed to South Korea by air and sea were 480 men from the 24th Infantry Division. It was named 'Task Force Smith' after its commanding officer. Not a fully-equipped fighting force, they were intended only as a 'show of force' to improve the morale of the retreating ROKA units and deter the NKPA from continuing the invasion and, at the same time, lead the enemy to believe that more US Army soldiers were already present in the country.

The US troops set up a blocking position south of the South Korean capital of Seoul, which had been captured by the NKPA on 28 June. One of the unit's officers informed his men: 'Those Commie bastards will turn and run when they find that they're up against our boys.' He went on to say: 'We'll be back in Seoul by the weekend.'

What is an RCT?

Regimental Combat Teams (RCTs) were temporary formations based on Marine or Army infantry regiments to which a range of support units were added. These include armour, signal and engineering units for missions of varying duration. Upon the completion of their assigned tasks, the supporting groups of the RCTs transfer back to the divisional level or corps levels, and the infantry regiments assume their standard table of organization (TO&Es). The Marine Corps continues to employ the label RCTs post-Korean War, whereas the US Army stopped using the term following the Korean War.

On 5 July some thirty-three T-34-85 medium tanks and their supporting truck-borne infantry overran and routed Task Force Smith within a time span of around six hours. It is doubtful that the NKPA troops even knew they were fighting American soldiers until they came across the dead, wounded and captured troops of Task Force Smith.

What's Next?

With the overrunning of Task Force Smith, the leading elements of the NKPA continued their southward advance towards the South Korean port city of Pusan, located on the south-eastern tip of the Korean Peninsula. It was South Korea's only deep-water port, and thus the gateway for American reinforcements and supply.

Additional elements of the 24th Infantry Division were rushed piecemeal into South Korea via Pusan in July 1950, tasked with setting up blocking positions to slow down the NKPA advance. However, the enemy overcame these blocking forces, costing the lives of approximately 4,000 men of the 24th Infantry Division.

On 2 August a regiment of the 24th Infantry Division, now supported by American medium tanks, successfully stopped the advance of a division of the NKPA at the South Korean port city of Masan. The town lay 35 miles west of Pusan. As the enemy withdrew, it would be hard hit by American air power.

Defending the Pusan Perimeter

Despite its first significant defeat, the NKPA continued to advance on Pusan. However, by this time there were elements of three US Army divisions – the 24th and 25th Infantry divisions along with the 1st Cavalry Division – present in South Korea. Also there were now five reorganized ROKA infantry divisions and a British Army infantry regiment within the Pusan Perimeter. In all, the number of UN ground troops within the Pusan Perimeter totalled about 100,000 men, mostly Americans and South Koreans.

As of September 1950, the US Army 2nd Infantry Division, the US Army 5th RCT and the British 27th Commonwealth Brigade had also arrived in Pusan. The number count of UN troops within the Pusan Perimeter now rose to about 180,000 men, not all combat troops. The estimated North Korean personnel count surrounding the Pusan Perimeter came in at 98,000 men.

Marine 'Fire Brigade'

For six weeks (4 August–18 September) the NKPA lay siege to the Pusan Perimeter, mounting attack after attack without success. Greatly aiding the commanding general of the EUSA in his defence of the Pusan Perimeter, American and South Korean code-breakers had decrypted the NKPA radio codes providing him with advance notice of many of the enemy's intentions.

To keep the NKPA off balance, the EUSA commander mounted a series of counteroffensives, some were more successful than others. A key player in these countermoves against the NKPA forces surrounding the Pusan Perimeter would be the approximately 4,000 men of the '1st Provisional Marine Brigade'. Activated on 7 July in Southern California, the formation arrived at Pusan on 2 August. The men of the brigade had trained hard the year before and had a great many combat-experienced officers and NCOs within the ranks.

Well-known author of military history Clay Blair pointed out in his book *The Forgotten War: America in Korea 1950–1953* that 'the [Marine] ranks were filled with physically tough young men who had joined the corps to fight, not to sightsee. The Marines had superior firepower in squads, platoons, and companies.' Reflecting the Marine unit's cohesion and experienced leadership, the EUSA commander saw the 1st Marine Provisional Brigade as his elite 'fire brigade' (back-up emergency force). They were to be employed wherever the threat to the Pusan Perimeter was the greatest.

Once in South Korea, the 1st Provisional Marine Brigade came under the command of Marine Brigadier General (BG) Edward A. Craig, who reached the rank of LTG in January 1951. The brigade had support from squadrons belonging to the First Marine Aircraft Wing (1st MAW). It, in turn, was subdivided into two Marine Aircraft Groups (MAGs): MAG-12 and MAG-33. The first strike carried out by the aircraft of the 1st MAW occurred on 3 August against a variety of ground targets.

The daylight-only fighter squadrons of the 1st MAW flew the prop-driven F4U-4B Corsair from US Navy aircraft carriers stationed off the coast of Korea. The night-fighter squadrons of the 1st MAW, flying out of Japan, operated both the F4U-5N and the new twin-engine, prop-driven F7F Tigercat. There was also another squadron that would operate out of the Pusan Perimeter equipped with prop-driven OY-2 light observation planes and piston-engine HO3S-1 helicopters.

It was the 1st Marine Division, with a personnel strength on paper of approximately 22,000 men, that MacArthur wanted for a future campaign. However, like the

---

The 1st Provisional Marine Brigade Background

As reflected in its title, the 1st Provisional Marine Brigade was an ad hoc unit formed at various times between 1912 and 1950 for specific missions. Upon finishing those missions, it went on to be deactivated and its men and equipment returned to their parent units. In the case of the brigade, it would be the 5th Regiment of the 1st Marine Division that formed its core with other support units added, such as Company A of the 1st (Marine) Tank Battalion. There were three infantry regiments in each Marine infantry division. Unlike the US Army, the Marine Corps never formed armoured divisions.

US Army, the Marine Corps had shrunk in size following its Second World War high of six full-strength divisions down to less than two half-strength divisions. On 19 July the Marine Corps therefore called up its reserves to bring the 1st Marine Division up to full strength as quickly as possible.

Into the Breach

Upon their arrival at Pusan, the 1st Provisional Marine Brigade was immediately trucked to Masan. The brigade joined the US Army 25th Infantry Division and the US Army 5th RCT, under the overall command of US Army Brigadier General William B. Kean. The three units became 'Task Force Kean', numbering about 20,000 men.

EUSA plans issued on 6 August called for Task Force Kean to move westward from their position near the port of Masan, then to secure the Chinju Pass near the South Korean city of Chinju and go on to secure a new main line as far as the Nam River. The primary purpose of the counteroffensive was to break up a suspected massing of enemy units near the Taegu area captured by the enemy on 20 July by forcing some of the NKPA formations southward to stop Task Force Kean's advance.

As Task Force Kean advanced on 7 August, the participating US Army units quickly became bogged down upon encountering the NKPA. Unbeknown to Task Force Kean, an enemy division had launched an assault of its own against the Pusan Perimeter on 7 August. Their attack was to be along the same general path that Task Force Kean had planned on using to obtain its objectives. The North Korean general in charge issued a statement to his troops before they advanced:

> Comrades, the enemy is demoralized. The task given to us is the liberation of Masan and Chinju and the annihilation of the remnants of the enemy. We have … accelerated the liberation of all Korea. However, the liberation of Chinju and Masan means the final battle to cut off the windpipe of the enemy. Comrades, this glorious task has fallen to our division! Men of the 6th Division, let us annihilate the enemy and distinguish ourselves!

Despite this collision of forces, the 1st Provisional Marine Brigade beat back the enemy units it encountered and continued to advance. In the book titled *Soldiers of the Sea* by Colonel Robert D. Heinl Jr, he summed up the impressions made on both the Marines and the NKPA after encountering each other in battle on that first day:

> The Marines got their first taste of the enemy. They found him spirited, tenacious, well-trained, and generously equipped with Russian gear. Used to having the campaign their own way, the North Koreans fought confidently, but reacted with considerable surprise when they found themselves facing troops

who gave no ground, hung on to their weapons, and brought in their wounded and dead.

Marine Air Support

One of the reasons for the Marines' success proved to be the close air support they received from their attack squadrons. In the first three days of fighting, they flew more than 110 sorties. They also managed to keep some of their aircraft overhead at all times to respond quickly when called to action. The Marines Corps' emphasis on close-in aerial support was to make up for its lack of heavy artillery.

To control Marine aircraft over the battlefield and spot for their artillery, the Marines' light observation planes carried forward air controllers (FACs). A Marine officer explained in a USMC historical publication the advantages provided by light observation planes:

In this type of terrain, the enemy was so adept at camouflage that most of the time high-performance aircraft were just too fast to get down and search out a target. We in the slower-moving aircraft were able to get down much lower, take our time in spotting a target, and then to stand off to one side or the other of the [bombing] run, and make sure the aircraft were hitting the correct targets. Too, we were using the same maps that the ground commanders were using. They were able to give us targets and pinpoint the targets with exact coordinates.

On 11 August, as the Marines continued their push forward, they came across the South Korean town of Kosong. To flush out any enemy troops that might be within the town, a barrage of Marine artillery fire straddled it. Unbeknown to the US infantrymen, the town contained an NKPA motorized unit that then attempted to flee.

Unluckily for the enemy, Marine F4U-4B Corsair fighters showed up at the same time and, upon witnessing the NKPA formation in flight, swooped down for the kill. From a Marine Corps historical publication is a passage describing what then occurred, referred to as the 'Kosong Turkey Shoot':

The Corsairs came screaming down in low-level strafing runs the entire length of the column for the purpose of bringing it to a halt. Vehicles crashed into one another or piled up in a ditch, while enemy troops scrambled for cover. The Soviet-made Jeeps and motorcycles were now sitting ducks for the F4-Us which worked over individual targets with rockets or 20mm fire. After the Marine planes had set about forty vehicles on fire, they were relieved by another flight of VMF-323 [Squadron] machines and Air Force F-51s [Mustangs] which added the finishing touches to the picture of destruction.

The US Army is in Trouble

By 12 August the 1st Provisional Marine Brigade had covered 29 miles in four days and caused heavy losses among the NKPA units that stood in its path. Its objectives were coming within reach when US Army Brigadier General William B. Kean ordered a reinforced battalion of the brigade back to the start line. NKPA units had severely beaten the US Army 5th RCT on 11 August, which had included the overrunning of all its artillery units.

Upon securing a great deal of the area, they found that the NKPA had departed. The next morning of 13 August, the Marines continued to search the surrounding area without encountering any enemy troops.

Any hope that Brigadier General Edward A. Craig had of continuing his advance were dashed that same day by the EUSA commander. He ordered the entire 1st Provisional Marine Brigade back to the start line on 13 August and the remainder of Task Force Kean on 14 August. On the latter date the EUSA commander ordered the Marines to move to a new location and prepare themselves to meet a growing enemy threat along the Naktong River.

From the official history of the Marine Corps during the Korean War is this passage by an officer regarding how upset many were at having to give up ground won at such a high cost: 'I found it difficult to see men, veterans of the last war, older guys, sitting by the side of the road crying. They just didn't give a hoot. They were just tired, disgusted. People just couldn't understand this part of the war.'

Task Force Kean was dissolved on 16 August without achieving any of its goals. Losses for the 1st Provisional Marine Brigade came in at 66 killed or died of wounds, 240 wounded and 9 missing in action presumed dead. The official Marine Corps' history of the Korean War estimated that the Marine air-ground team killed or injured 1,900 of the enemy during its time with Task Force Kean.

Another Emergency Response

North-west of Masan there was an area referred to as the 'Naktong Bulge' that formed part of the Naktong River. From the official US Army history of the Korean War is the following passage describing the area, the site and its importance to the defence of the Pusan Perimeter:

> Along the [Pusan] Perimeter, the most important terrain feature for both the United Nations and the North Koreans – helping the former and hindering the latter – was the Naktong River, the second-largest river in Korea. It formed a huge moat in front of almost three-fourths of the [Pusan] Perimeter. Its numerous great folds and bends resembled a huge snake contracting its length before coiling. Along its lower course, the river is generally from one-quarter to half a mile wide and more than six feet deep.

On 6 August an NKPA division crossed the Naktong River in strength at the Naktong Bulge. Defending that part of the Pusan Perimeter was 'Task Force Hill' consisting of elements of the US Army 2nd Infantry Division and the US Army 24th Infantry Division. They failed to stop the NKPA advance, and the EUSA commander threw into the fray additional elements of the US Army 2nd Division as well as the 25th Infantry Division and the 1st Provisional Marine Brigade on 15 August.

A British Army officer present on 15 August was anxious that the NKPA advance at the Naktong Bulge might collapse the Pusan Perimeter. His faith in the eventual outcome changed upon observing the arrival of the 1st Provisional Marine Brigade. He would state:

> I realize my expression of hope is unsound, but these Marines have the swagger, confidence and hardness that must have been in Stonewall Jackson's Army of the Shenandoah. They remind me of the Coldstreams [Guard] at Dunkerque. Upon this thin line of reasoning, I cling to the hope of victory.

The Counterattack Begins

US Army reinforcement and the 1st Provisional Marine Brigade, attached to the 24th Infantry Division, began counterattacking the NKPA along the Pusan Perimeter on 17 August. The fighting was at the time referred to by the American military as the 'First Battle of the Naktong Bulge'.

In the early evening of 17 August, the Marines encountered for the first time in battle the much-feared enemy T-34-85 medium tanks. Four of them appeared in sight of the Marines in their hilltop position. Marine aircraft quickly arrived overhead and managed to damage one of the enemy tanks and scatter the accompanying infantry.

The Marines' 3.5in rocket-launchers and 75mm recoilless rifles damaged another enemy tank. As the third enemy tank rounded a corner, it too was hit by rocket and recoilless rifle rounds. It skidded off the road and would be finished off by a platoon of five Marine M26 Pershing medium tanks that also destroyed the last remaining enemy tank.

The 1st Marine Provisional Brigade had arrived in South Korea with a company of M26 medium tanks and two M4A3 medium tanks fitted with the horizontal volute suspension system (HVSS) armed with 105mm howitzers and equipped with dozer blades.

When the NKPA attacked the Marine Corps' hilltop positions in strength on the night of 17 August, it would be the 4.2in mortars that decided the fighting, as appears in a passage taken from the US Marine Corps' official history of the conflict:

> The 1st Battalion [of the 1st Provisional Marine Brigade] was receiving a terrifically heavy counterattack. Our [heavy weapons] company was zeroed on the hill and valley in front of the battalion. When notified of this attack, we began

firing our prearranged barrages. Later, where only one of these barrages had fallen, they counted 120 dead North Koreans with 12 cart-mounted machine guns, who had been massed in this little gulley behind the hill, a ridge in front of the battalion that would have caused them considerable trouble.

By the morning of 18 August, the enemy attacks began to weaken. The US Army commanding officer ordered that his US Army units and the 1st Provisional Marine Brigade resume their advance, to take place under the covering fire of American aircraft, artillery and tanks.

By that afternoon, the enemy had had enough and in a panic-stricken rout tried to flee back across the Naktong River under heavy fire. Marine pilots reported: 'The enemy was killed in such numbers that the river was definitely discoloured with blood.' So ended the First Battle of the Naktong Bulge.

Round Two

The NKPA realized that it needed to act quickly before the UN forces within the Pusan Perimeter grew strong enough to go on the offensive and break through their lines. On 20 August the enemy's senior leadership decided to employ the bulk of its forces to mount five separate attacks on the Pusan Perimeter to commence on 1 September.

The enemy decided that the US Army 2nd Infantry Division, defending a portion of the Naktong River, was a weak spot in the Pusan Perimeter. The NKPA, therefore, committed four divisions to attack that US Army division. The result would be the 'Second Battle of the Naktong Bulge'.

A US Army report from 1952 describes how the NKPA attacked: 'The common tactical maneuver of the North Korean Army forces at the time was a strong frontal attack to fix the enemy in place, and then a double envelopment to encircle and annihilate him.'

As with the First Battle of the Naktong Bulge, the enemy quickly overran the US Army's forward defensive lines. Once again, the EUSA commander had to make the embarrassing decision to employ the 1st Provisional Marine Brigade to restore the US Army's front-line positions.

A problem that arose regarding committing the 1st Provisional Marine Brigade to the Second Battle of the Naktong Bulge centred on a plan of MacArthur's. He wanted to seize the enemy-occupied port city of Inchon on the west coast of Korea. The purpose: to cut the NKPA supply lines and allow the UN forces to break out of the Pusan Perimeter.

For that amphibious landing at Inchon, MacArthur wanted the 1st Provisional Marine Brigade reabsorbed by its parent unit, the 1st Marine Division, as the latter was to be the spearhead of his operation. However, MacArthur's staff agreed that the

EUSA commander could keep the 1st Provisional Marine Brigade until midnight of 5 September before being pulled for use in the Inchon operation.

Forward Once Again

On 3 September the 1st Provisional Marine Brigade, now attached to the US Army 2nd Infantry Division, advanced once again in the face of heavy enemy fire. When the NKPA troops opened fire on the Marines, it resulted in the wrath of their supporting arms coming down on them. This included tank fire, artillery bombardments and aircraft dropping napalm canisters engulfing them in flaming sheets of fire.

A US Army colonel was observing the close air support provided to the Marines. He would write to US Army General Matthew Ridgway, then in Washington DC:

> The Marines on our left were a sight to behold. Not only was their equipment superior or equal to ours, but they had squadrons of air in direct support. They used it like artillery. It was 'Hey, Joe – This is Smitty – Knock the left off that ridge in front of Item Company.' They had it day and night . . . General, we just have to have air support like that, or we may as well disband the infantry and join the Marines.

On the night of 3 September, the Marine infantrymen no doubt expected a major attack on their hilltop positions. As a precaution, the unit's engineers had sowed a large number of anti-personnel mines, wired hand grenades and blocks of TNT along the flanks of the Marines' positions.

The 1st Provisional Marine Brigade's supporting squadron of night-fighters, flying in from Japan, flew six close air support missions that night. In combination with a stormy night, the enemy, to everyone's surprise, did not mount a nighttime attack.

The lack of aggressiveness on the part of the NKPA on the night of 3 September appeared the next morning when the enemy troops decided to withdraw in the face of the American advance in what began a disorderly rout. On the night of 4 September, the enemy once more failed to launch their typical assault on the Marines' hilltop positions.

On 5 September heavy rain kept the Marines' air support grounded. The enemy took advantage of the situation and mounted a daylight attack on the 1st Provisional Marine Brigade that included three tanks. That attack would be beaten off at the last minute by Marine reinforcements, as well as their 81mm mortar fire and US Army artillery support.

The Closing Act

The enlisted men and officers of the 1st Provisional Marine Brigade wanted to pursue the enemy back to their crossing-point on the Naktong River. However, that was not to be as they were to be pulled back to the port of Pusan by truck and train, arriving on 7 September. The US Army units that remained behind continued to attack, bringing the Second Battle of the Naktong Bulge to a successful conclusion on 12 September.

During the three days of fighting for the Naktong Bulge, the 1st Provisional Marine Brigade lost 148 men killed in action and 730 wounded, of whom 15 later died from their wounds. Nine were listed as missing in action, with seven of those later confirmed as killed in action.

To prepare for its position in the upcoming landing at Inchon as part of the 1st Marine Division, the 1st Provisional Marine Brigade would be re-equipped and provided with 1,136 replacements. Also, a regiment of 3,000 South Korean Marines (armed with leftover Japanese Army small arms) was attached to the brigade. On 11 September the men of the 1st Provisional Marine Brigade began boarding the ships that would form part of MacArthur's Inchon invasion fleet.

In the early-morning darkness of 25 June 1950, the North Korean People's Army (NKPA) invaded South Korea. It began with an artillery bombardment followed by the advance of 150 Soviet Army-supplied T-34-85 medium tanks, with an example pictured here. Not having any suitable anti-tank weapons, the Republic of Korea Army (ROKA) quickly fled. (*Pierre-Olivier Buan*)

Besides the T-34-85 medium tank, the Soviet Union also provided approximately seventy-five examples of the SU-76M assault gun to the NKPA with an example pictured here. The establishment of an armoured force within the NKPA began under the guidance of both Soviet and Red Chinese military advisors in 1948, with the NKPA standing up its first armoured brigade the following year. (*Christophe Vallier*)

Pictured is the man behind the June 1950 invasion of South Korea, Kim Il-sung, premier of North Korea. He arrived on the international stage as part of the Soviet Army to accept the surrender of the Japanese occupiers on August 1948. At the time, he held the rank of major in the Soviet Army. Of proven loyalty, he was appointed by Stalin to lead North Korea in September 1948. (*NA*)

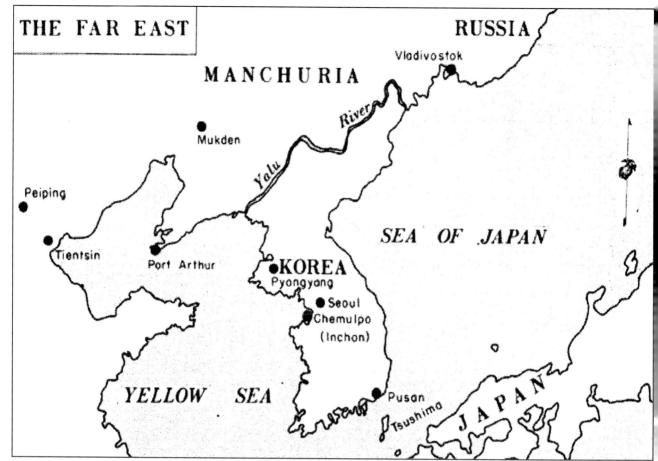

THE FAR EAST

RUSSIA

MANCHURIA

Vladivostok

Mukden

Yalu *River*

Peiping

Tientsin

Port Arthur

SEA OF JAPAN

●KOREA
Pyongyang

●Seoul
Chemulpo
(Inchon)

YELLOW SEA

Pusan
Tsushima

JAPAN

The Korean Peninsula extends for around 600 miles north to south with a width of approximately 120 to 200 miles. It shares an 850-mile border with Red China, much of it along the Yalu River. It also shares an 11-mile border with the Soviet Union along the Tumen River. The capital of North Korea is Pyongyang, and Seoul is that of South Korea. (USMC)

Before its departure from South Korea in the summer of 1949, the US Army transferred a great deal of military equipment to the Republic of Korea Army (ROKA). The South Korean soldier pictured here has an M1 Garand rifle with an attached M7 grenade-launcher. He also wears a US Army helmet liner and some American web gear. (NA)

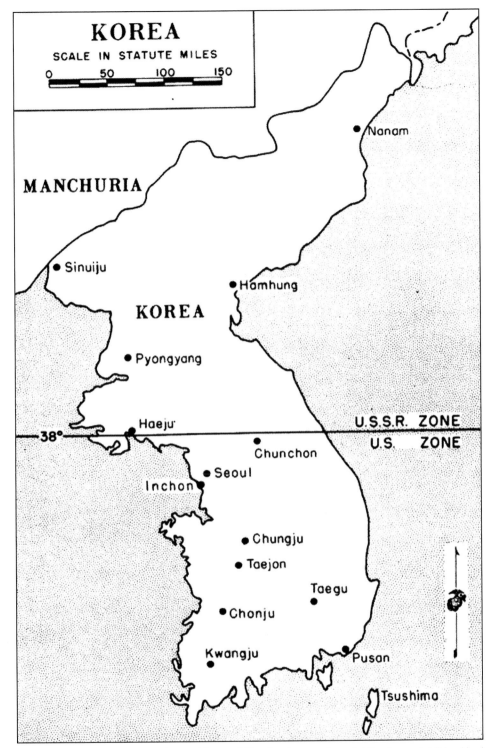

In this illustration appears the 38th Parallel, an arbitrary 190-mile demarcation dividing line established in August 1945 and approved by both American President Harry S. Truman and Soviet Premier Joseph Stalin. It supposedly marked the temporary spheres of influence of the US and Soviet armies in Korea until such time that the Korean people could elect their leadership under United Nations (UN) supervision. (*USMC*)

Due to concerns regarding Syngman Rhee, the South Korean president, and his strong anti-communist views, the American government and military leadership decided not to provide the ROKA with any offensive weapons such as tanks for fear that he might attack North Korea and drag the United States into a conflict it did not want. The ROKA did receive obsolete US Army M1 57mm anti-tank guns like the one pictured. (NA)

The only armoured fighting vehicles the ROKA received from the US Army were thirty-seven examples of the M8 Light Armored Car (pictured here) and a small number of M3 Half-Track Personnel Carriers. The ROKA itself came about on 15 December 1948. Before that it consisted only of eight constabulary (internal security) regiments established as a back-up to the National Police force. (NA)

ROKA soldiers are shown here emplacing a US Army anti-tank mine. Upon the opening advance of the NKPA, the poorly-trained and poorly-equipped South Korean Army divisions quickly disintegrated and fled southward. The South Korean capital of Seoul fell to the invaders on the fourth day of the war. The 500 American soldiers of the Korean Military Advisory Group (KMAG) were evacuated by air. (NA)

(**Above, left**) Much to the surprise of the North Korean premier, on 27 June 1950 the UN called for all its members to 'furnish such assistance to the Republic of Korea as may be necessary to repel the armed attack and to restore international peace and security in that area.' That same day American President Harry S. Truman (seen here) authorized American air and naval support of South Korea. *(NA)*

(**Above, right**) The man that President Truman entrusted with overseeing the air and naval support of South Korea was US Army General Douglas MacArthur, seen here in a 1945 photograph with his well-known corn-cob pipe. MacArthur had become the Commander-in-Chief, Far East Command (FECOM) in 1947. On 8 July 1950 he was appointed Chief of the United Nations Command (UNC) and given control of the ROKA on 14 July 1950. *(NA)*

(**Opposite**) An ROKA soldier is seen here comforting a wounded comrade. To decide if American ground forces were required, General MacArthur flew to South Korea on 29 June 1950. What he found was chaos. He wrote to the Joint Chiefs of Staff (JCS): 'The only assurance for the holding of the present line, and the ability to regain later the lost ground is through the introduction of US ground combat forces.' *(NA)*

(**Above**) General MacArthur and his staff believed that a US Army unit consisting of only 540 men from the 24th Infantry Division named Task Force Smith would be enough to deter the NKPA from continuing their invasion. Task Force Smith's soldiers were flown to South Korea from Japan aboard six United States Air Force (USAF) C-54 Skymaster cargo planes on 1 July 1950. Pictured here is a USAF C-54. (*NA*)

(**Opposite, above**) Because the bulk of Task Force Smith was flown into South Korea by plane, it could only take its lightest weapons. Included among its anti-tank weapons were the M1/M1A1 2.36in Rocket-Launchers, best known by their popular nickname of the 'Bazooka'. The initial model is pictured here, entering service in 1942, with the M1A1 version introduced into use the following year. (*NA*)

(**Opposite, below**) The only other dedicated anti-tank weapons that Task Force Smith brought to South Korea were two units of the M20 75mm Recoilless Rifle, with an example pictured here. Introduced into US Army service during the final few months of the Second World War, it weighed 114.5lb. It had a length of 6ft 10in and fired from the same tripod used for the .30 Calibre M1917A1 Heavy Machine Gun. (*USMC*)

(**Above**) Joining the soldiers of Task Force Smith upon their arrival in South Korea on 1 July were 134 men of an artillery battery belonging to the 24th Infantry Division that was already in-country. Pictured here is a preserved M101A1 105mm howitzer as would have been used by Task Force Smith. The only other indirect fire weapons possessed by Task Force Smith were two 4.2in M2 mortars. (*NA*)

(**Opposite, above**) On 5 July, Task Force Smith was quickly overrun and routed near the South Korean city of Osan by an NKPA tank regiment accompanied by infantry, in the process of which the Americans lost 150 men and most of their equipment. Pictured here is a soldier from Task Force Smith with his hands tied behind his back and shot in the head; he had been captured by the enemy. (*NA*)

(**Opposite, below**) The overrunning of Task Force Smith demonstrated that the NKPA was not to be cowed by the presence of American soldiers. MacArthur and his staff had the Eighth Army, based in Japan, funneled in additional men and equipment as quickly as possible from its four under-strength infantry divisions. Among the first US Army tanks deployed to South Korea were M24 light tanks, with an example pictured here. (*NA*)

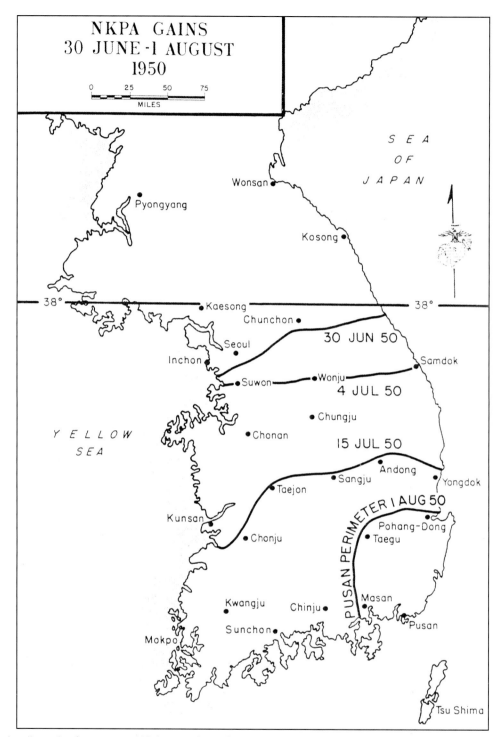

NKPA GAINS
30 JUNE-1 AUGUST
1950

0   25   50   75
MILES

SEA OF JAPAN

Wonsan

Pyongyang

Kosong

38°   38°
Kaesong
Chunchon
30 JUN 50
Seoul
Inchon   Samdok
Suwon   Wonju
4 JUL 50
Chungju
Chonan
15 JUL 50
Andong
Sangju   Yongdok
Taejon
PUSAN PERIMETER 1 AUG 50
Kunsan
Pohang-Dong
Chonju   Taegu

YELLOW SEA

Kwangju   Chinju   Masan
Sunchon   Pusan
Mokpo

Tsu Shima

Despite the dispatch of ever more US Army units to South Korea in July 1950, the NKPA advanced ever further into South Korea, as shown on this map. By 1 August the surviving UN forces were confined to an area approximately 90 miles in length from north to south and around 60 miles from east to west. The area came to be known as the 'Pusan Perimeter'. Pusan was South Korea's major deep-water port. (USMC)

A pre-Korean War parade by Marine Corps M4 series tanks. Like its US Army counterparts, the 1st Marine Division was badly under-strength in June 1950, having only one of its three infantry regiments and its single artillery regiment on active service. The other two regiments had been deactivated following the Second World War. (*USMC*)

(**Opposite, above left**) Anticipating the commitment of American military ground forces to the Korean conflict, General Clifton B. Gates (pictured), the commandant of the Marine Corps (1948–51), on 28 June 1950 ordered the US 1st Marine Division to prepare itself to go to war. Two days later, President Truman authorized the deployment of American ground troops for combat in Korea. (*USMC*)

(**Opposite, above right**) General Gates had the 1st Provisional Marine Brigade activated on 7 July 1950 for early departure to Korea in place of the not yet fully-staffed 1st Marine Division. The brigade was an ad hoc unit raised for temporary assignments. The commander of the 5th Marine Regiment, the core of the brigade, was Lieutenant Colonel Raymond L. Murray, pictured here, who had served with distinction in the Second World War. (*USMC*)

(**Opposite, below**) The assistant division commander of the 1st Marine Division in 1949 was Brigadier General Edward A. Craig, a much-decorated Second World War veteran. Upon the forming of the 1st Provisional Marine Brigade in July 1950, he assumed its command. Craig is seen in this photograph with South Korean President Syngman Rhee at an award ceremony. (*USMC*)

(**Above**) The 1st Provisional Marine Brigade went to Korea equipped with the M20 3.5in Rocket-Launcher with an example pictured here in the hands of its two-man crew. The M20 was nicknamed the 'Super Bazooka' and was in theory able to penetrate 11in of steel armour. For ease of transport, it folded in half when not in use. (*USMC*)

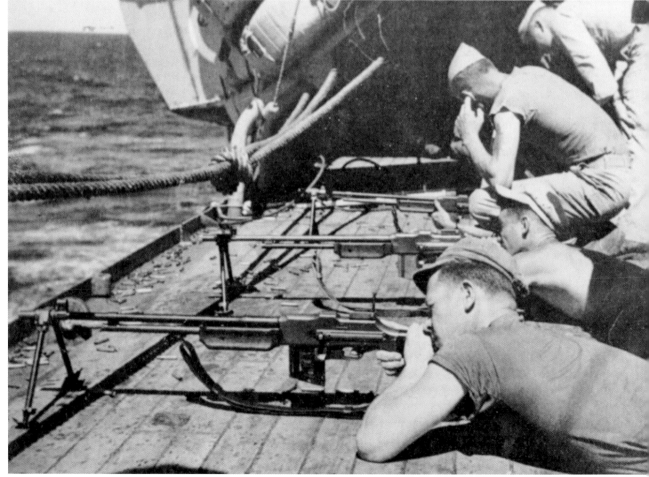

(**Opposite, above**) Another piece of new equipment provided to the 1st Provisional Marine Brigade before its departure was the 46-ton M26 medium tank pictured here. Assigned the official nickname 'Pershing', it replaced most of the M4A3 medium tanks armed with the 105mm howitzer employed by the Marines. The Pershing tanks of the brigade belonged to Company A of the 1st Tank Battalion. (*Pierre-Olivier Buan*)

(**Opposite, below**) On 14 July, the 1st Provisional Marine Brigade set sail from San Diego, California. Pictured here are Marines training with their Browning Automatic Rifles (BARs) while at sea. When General MacArthur found out that the still en route brigade was only at its peacetime staffing levels, he informed the Joint Chiefs of Staff (JCS) that he required it to be brought up to full strength as quickly as possible. (*USMC*)

(**Above**) On board one of the ships bound for South Korea are some of the men of the 1st Provisional Marine Brigade, attending a training class on the M1919A4 .30 Calibre Air-Cooled Light Machine Gun. On 19 July, in response to General MacArthur's requirement for the mobilization of the entire 1st Marine Division for a future campaign, Marine Reserves were called up. (*USMC*)

Men of the 1st Provisional Marine Brigade are seen here marching through the streets of Pusan on 2 August after disembarking from their transport ships. Originally the brigade was going to billet in Japan, but the continuing deterioration of the military situation in South Korea resulted in their ships being redirected en route to South Korea to shore up the American Eighth Army (EUSA) in defence of the Pusan Perimeter. (USMC)

The 1st Provisional Marine Brigade was an air-ground team. The brigade's air element consisted of various squadrons from the 1st Marine Air Wing (1st MAW). In this picture, we see the US Navy escort carrier USS Badoeng Strait (CVE-116) bringing gull-winged F4U Corsairs from three different attack squadrons to Pusan. At the very front of the flight deck is an HO3S-1 helicopter. (US Navy)

The mainstay of the various 1st MAW attack squadrons that served during the Korean War would be the F4U-4B model of the Corsair, as shown here. The day-only fighter received power from a 2,100hp engine which gave it a top speed of almost 450 mph, a climb rate of 3,870ft per second and a range of around 1,000 miles. It could reach an altitude of 41,500ft. (*USMC*)

(**Above**) The F4U-4B Corsairs flew off US Navy carriers, as well as airfields in Korea. Armed with six .50 calibre machine guns they had a payload capability of eight 5in rockets and up to 4,000lb of other ordnance. (*USMC*)

(**Opposite, above**) Among the variants of the Corsair that saw combat during the Korean War was a night-fighter version seen here labelled the F4U-5N. The aircraft can be identified by the bulbous radar radome on its right wing, which appears in this image. The aircraft flew both interdiction missions and combat air patrols against enemy prop-driven aircraft operating at night. (*USMC*)

(**Opposite, below**) Another night-fighter employed by the Marine Corps during the early stages of the Korean War was the F7F-3N Tigercat, with an example pictured here. Of the 364 constructed, only 60 came off the production lines as dedicated night-fighters, with a two-man crew and the radar located in the aircraft's nose. Armament consisted of four 20mm automatic cannon. (*USMC*)

Among the various squadrons of the 1st MAW supporting the 1st Provisional Marine Brigade in Korea would be Observation Squadron 6 (VMO-6). It had four HO3S-1 helicopters, with an example pictured here, and four OY-2 single-engine, prop-driven, OY-2 observation planes. The Marine Corps had pioneered the use of helicopters beginning in 1947. (USMC)

FIRE EXTINGUISHER INSIDE

Seen here in the pilot's seat of an HO3S-1 helicopter is then Captain Victor A. Armstrong. A decorated Second World War pilot, he was commander of VMO-6 when it arrived in South Korea in August 1950. The HO3S-1 had a cruising speed of 85 mph and a range of around 260 miles. Among its many roles were as a command and control platform, as an artillery spotter and as a reconnaissance aircraft. (USMC)

On 12 August, the bulk of the 1st Provisional Marine Brigade was pulled from the forefront of Task Force Kean and sent rearward to rescue three US Army artillery batteries overrun by the NKPA the previous day. By the time the Marines arrived, the enemy had already vacated the area. Two Marine riflemen remain on alert in this picture. (*USMC*)

(**Opposite, above**) Like the HO3S-1 helicopters of VM0-6, the two-man OY-2 Sentinel light observation planes performed a variety of roles during the Korean War. Especially valuable was its performance as a forward air controller (FAC) and artillery spotter. Almost 4,000 were built in various versions from 1942 through to 1945. The Marine Corps eventually acquired 152 units. (*USMC*)

(**Opposite, below**) On 3 August, eight Marine Corps Corsairs from a US Navy aircraft carrier conducted the first Marine offensive action of the war, attacking NKPA positions. The 1st Provisional Marine Brigade's ground elements initially entered into combat on 10 August as part of the EUSA's first counteroffensive referred to as Task Force Kean. Pictured here are two Marines: the prone soldier is armed with a BAR, and the Marine in the foreground with an M2 carbine. (*USMC*)

(**Opposite, above**) Task Force Kean would continue until 16 August. On 15 August the 1st Provisional Marine Brigade was committed to a counterattack along with US Army units due to an NKPA attack that had broken through US Army lines along the Naktong River. The subsequent fighting came to be known as the First Battle of the Naktong Bulge. Pictured here is a Marine Corps M26 Pershing tank in Korea. (*USMC*)

(**Opposite, below**) It was during the First Battle of the Naktong Bulge that Marine tankers of Company A of the 1st Marine Tank Battalion faced combat with T-34-85 tanks of the NKPA. Four enemy tanks advancing towards the Marines' front-line positions on 17 August were engaged by four M26 Pershing tanks that quickly destroyed them without any losses to themselves. Pictured here are two of the four enemy tanks destroyed that day. (*USMC*)

(**Above**) Besides the Marine Corps tankers' contribution to the First Battle of the Naktong Bulge, the 11th Marine (Artillery) Regiment took a heavy toll on the NKPA, as it would throughout the Korean War. Shown here is an M101A1 105mm howitzer. The weapon fired a 33lb high-explosive shell to a maximum range of approximately 12,000 yards, or approximately 7 miles. (*USMC*)

(**Opposite, above**) An important weapon in every Marine infantry company was the M1 81mm Mortar pictured here in action during the Korean War. It fired a 6.8lb high-explosive shell up to 3,290 yards. It had a sustained rate of fire of around eighteen rounds per minute and, for a very short time, it could fire anywhere between thirty and thirty-five rounds per minute. (*USMC*)

(**Above**) The largest mortar employed by the Marine Corps during the Korean War was officially labelled the M2 4.2in (107mm) Chemical Mortar and unofficially nicknamed the 'four-deuce'. It fired a 25.5lb round to a maximum range of 4,400 yards. Due to its size and weight of 4,950lb, it was a far less flexible weapon than the smaller and lighter M1 81mm mortar. (*USMC*)

(**Opposite, below**) By the time of the Second Battle of the Naktong Bulge (1 to 12 September 1950), many of the original combat-experienced soldiers of the NKPA had been killed. In their place were less well-trained inexperienced North Korean soldiers, as well as South Korean civilians pressed into service with the NKPA. (*NA*)

Following combat, Marines are seen here examining a captured 7.62mm DP 1928 machine gun supplied to the NKPA by the Soviet Army from its massive stockpiles of weapons built up during the Second World War. A US Army report noted early in the Korean War that the NKPA attacked 'our hill positions with hand-carried weapons, relying heavily on the machine gun, and slightly less on the mortar'. (*USMC*)

(**Opposite, above**) When the 1st Provisional Marine Brigade arrived in Pusan on 2 August, Company A of the 1st Tank Battalion brought along two M4A3 medium tanks armed with 105mm howitzers. These rode on a Horizontal Volute Spring System (HVSS), as seen on the vehicle pictured here. They were also fitted with bulldozer blade kits (not pictured). (*Author's collection*)

(**Opposite, below**) A single M32A1B3 armoured recovery vehicle (ARV) based on the chassis of the M4A3(76)W medium tank riding on an HVSS as shown here was typically assigned to each Marine Corps' tank company. Fully capable of recovering M4 series medium tanks, it had a more difficult time in dealing with the larger and heavier M26 Pershing medium tanks. (*USMC*)

Among the towed anti-tank guns provided to the NKPA by the Soviet Army was the 45mm Model 1942 pictured here. During the Second World War, almost 11,000 units were produced. Its barrel was 10ft 2in in length and the gun had a maximum muzzle velocity of 2,854ft per second. Unable to penetrate the frontal armour on the M26 Pershing tank, the gun could nevertheless penetrate the M26's more thinly-armoured portions. *(Pierre-Olivier Buan)*

Prodded by the introduction of more heavily-armoured late-war German tanks, the Red Army introduced the 57mm ZIS-2 1943 anti-tank gun. It, too, was supplied to the NKPA. The standard armour-piercing (AP) round with a muzzle velocity of 3,300ft per second it could, in theory, penetrate 3.1in of armour sloped at 50 degrees. *(Vladimir Yakubov)*

The 1st Provisional Marine Brigade withdrew from the Pusan Perimeter on 7 September 1950. The brigade would return to the port of Pusan and board ships on 11 September 1950, intending to join up with a US Navy fleet off the North Korean-occupied port of Inchon. Upon arrival off Inchon it again became part of the 1st Marine Division. Pictured here are Marine M26 Pershing tanks on a US Navy Landing Ship Tank (LST) heading towards Inchon. (USMC)

Chapter Two

The Battles for Inchon and Seoul

A few days after the North Korean invasion of South Korea began, MacArthur's staff became aware of a contingency plan authored by a civilian staffer in the Pentagon. It had envisioned a North Korean invasion of South Korea in which the ROKA would be forced to fall back to Pusan. It suggested that American military forces go to Pusan, followed by an amphibious landing behind the enemy's forward positions to cut their supply lines.

When the Pentagon contingency plan arrived at MacArthur's headquarters in Tokyo, MacArthur and his staff embraced it as their own. Steps were quickly taken to decide the optimum landing location. MacArthur and his staff then consulted with Marine representatives about their proposed amphibious invasion on 4 July.

On 10 July, MacArthur made the first of several requests to the JCS that the 1st Marine Division be transferred to his command. One read: 'Most urgently request reconsideration of decision … it is an absolutely vital development to accomplish a decisive stroke and if not made available will necessitate a much more costly and longer operational effort both in blood and expense.'

MacArthur has a Plan

MacArthur selected the port city of Inchon, then occupied by NKPA forces, for the amphibious invasion point. Located on the north-western shore of South Korea, Inchon was the country's second-largest port. Nearby was Kimpo airfield, the largest and most modern in Korea. Once Inchon was secured, the invading forces could push on to recapture the South Korean capital of Seoul, located 20 miles east of Inchon and 30 miles south of the 38th Parallel.

MacArthur explained his reasoning for seizing Inchon and Seoul:

I would completely paralyze the enemy's supply system – coming and going. This in turn will paralyze the fighting power of the troops that now face Walker [at the Pusan Perimeter]. Without munitions and food, they will soon be helpless and disorganized, and can easily be overpowered by our smaller but well-supplied forces.

Without the JCS's confirmation that he could have the 1st Marine Division, MacArthur proposed that the 1st Cavalry Division lead an Inchon landing code-named Operation BLUEHEARTS scheduled for 22 July. That operation had to be quickly cancelled on 10 July as the division was by that time needed to strengthen the Pusan Perimeter.

On 23 July MacArthur proposed another Inchon landing using the US Army 2nd Infantry Division and elements of a Marine regiment. That Marine unit would later become the 1st Marine Provisional Brigade. Unfortunately, they too were required at the Pusan Perimeter to prevent the NKPA from breaking through.

Not Everybody is On Board

MacArthur's selection of Inchon faced strenuous objections from almost everybody from the US Navy to the JCS. Inchon's terrain and a tidal range exceeding 30ft – one of the highest in the world – made any landing extremely difficult. Also, the harbour was only accessible via a narrow channel, easily blocked by a sunken vessel. All suggested that the NKPA would anticipate the landing site and might have already sowed both moored and magnetic mines throughout the harbour. The weather might also be a problem as the landing would take place during the height of the typhoon season.

On 23 August, the senior leaders of the US Far East Command (FECOM) presented their objections to MacArthur. He answered as described in a Marine Corps' historical publication titled *U.S. Marine Operations in Korea, 1950–1953*:

> Speaking with eloquence, he declared that the natural obstacles and practical difficulties of the proposed Inchon operation were more than balanced in the strategic scale by the psychological advantages of a bold stroke. About 90 percent of the NNKPA forces were fighting in the Pusan Perimeter. A combined offensive by the [newly-raised] X Corps and the EUSA would have the effect of placing the enemy between the hammer and anvil.

MacArthur ended his forty-five-minute speech with: 'We shall land at Inchon, and I shall crush them!' By the end of the meeting, those present acquiesced to MacArthur's plans by not continuing to harbour serious doubts about its chances of success.

As events unfolded, a captured high-ranking NKPA officer would later confess that he and other officers had heard rumours of a possible landing by the American military along the west coast of Korea, including Inchon. The Soviet Union warned the North Korean premier Kim Il-sung of what was going to happen, but he did not send reinforcements to Inchon. The NKPA, however, had constructed a great many fortifications around Inchon for reinforcements to occupy if called upon.

Set in Motion

For the landing, code-named Operation CHROMITE, the bulk of the 1st Marine Division (Reinforced) was hurriedly assembled from forces in Southern California as well as shipboard elements scattered across the Mediterranean. Two of the division's three infantry regiments – the 1st and 5th – plus a Marine Air Wing and amphibious support were set in motion to Japan between 10 and 22 August.

Also assigned to the Inchon landing was the US Army 7th Infantry Division. Due to a shortage of US Army reinforcements, almost half of the troops were poorly-trained ROKA soldiers. Both the 1st Marine Division and the US Army's 7th Infantry Division fell under the command of X Corps activated on 26 August 1950.

MacArthur did not appoint the leading Marine general on the scene to command X Corps, but instead his chief of staff, US Army Major General Edward M. Almond, who had no experience in amphibious operations. Almond was promoted to lieutenant general in February 1951.

On 1 September, the US Navy conducted a reconnaissance mission of Inchon's approaches and the harbour itself. Elements of the Marine 1st Division began departing from Japan by ship in stages, beginning on 5 September, so as not arouse suspicion. On 10 September both US Navy and Marine aircraft began a series of preliminary attacks on the Inchon area.

The Players

The 1st Marine Provisional Brigade departed Pusan on 13 September to rejoin its parent unit, the 1st Marine Division, on board US Navy ships near Inchon. For the invasion of Inchon the 1st and 5th Marine regiments were augmented with additional companies detached from Marine and US Army divisional support units to form the 1st and 5th Regimental Combat Teams, each with a personnel strength of around 4,000 men.

On 13 September, the US Navy commenced shore bombardment of the Inchon area. The plans called for the Marines of RCT-1 and RCT-5 to land at Inchon on 15 September and quickly advance towards Seoul. In command of the 1st Marine Division since June 1950 was Major General Oliver P. Smith, a highly-decorated veteran of the Second World War.

The Invasion Unfolds

Before the main landings at Inchon harbour could take place, the Marines of the 1st Division had to secure the NKPA-fortified island of Wolmi-do that dominated the harbour area. A Marine infantry battalion, assisted by ten medium tanks, was assigned the capture of the island. The landing began early on the morning of 15 September, and the island fell within forty-five minutes. An anticipated NKPA counterattack across a causeway that connected the island to the port city never materialized.

A Marine Corsair pilot involved in the aerial attacks on Wolmi-do recalled the following in a USMC historical publication:

> … several North Korean military vehicles were flushed out. Evidently, the enemy drivers believed that a moving target would be harder to hit. Perrin said that they got their Corsairs as low and slow as they could and literally chased the vehicles up and down streets and around corners in the island's small industrial sector. Eventually, all the vehicles felt the wrath of the blue fighters.

Due to Inchon's harbour and beach configuration as well as the tides, the 1st Marine Division's main landing would not commence until the early evening of 15 September. The Marines were to have only two hours of daylight to attain their objectives and take up defensive positions to foil any NKPA counterattacks that night.

The Marines were transported to their landing areas by US Navy landing craft of various types. There were also Marine Corps LVTs (Landing Vehicles, Tracked), nicknamed 'amtracs'. The latter were escorted to shore by a battalion of US Army LVT(A)-4s, LVTs armed with a turret-mounted 75mm howitzer. Lieutenant General Almond, the X Corps commander, stunned the Marine Corps' senior officers present when he asked if the amtracs could float on the water.

There had been little information available on enemy forces that might be at Inchon. The best estimate had put them at 1,500 to 2,000 men. As events transpired, it soon became apparent that they were insufficient in both numbers and weapons to pose any serious threat to the Marines of RCT-1 and RCT-5. That proved extremely fortunate for the 1st Marine Division, as their landings soon became very disorganized. An example of this appears in a passage from a USMC historical publication:

> Since currents and smoke fought relentlessly against tractors [LVTs] seaward of the line of departure, not all the vehicles could find the control ship. If they did, it was next to impossible to come in close enough to get instructions shouted from the bridge. Thus, many wave commanders, amtrac officers, and infantry leaders gave orders to head shoreward on their own initiative. They went in with waves and fragments of waves, displaying the kind of leadership that made the operation an overwhelming success in spite of the obstacles.

The Next Step

By midnight of 15 September, there were approximately 13,000 Marines ashore. In overrunning the city Marine casualties were very light, with only 21 dead, 1 missing in action and 174 wounded.

On the morning of 16 September, the 1st and 5th Marine regiments advanced in two columns along either side of the highway and railroad tracks that connected Inchon to Seoul. The 1st Marine Regiment was on the right and the 5th Marine

Regiment on the left, with the Marines of the 11th (Artillery) Regiment following and in support of both Marine (Infantry) regiments. The third infantry regiment (the 7th Marine Regiment) that made up the 1st Marine Division would not arrive at Inchon until 17 September as it was still en route from Japan when the Inchon landing began.

MacArthur declared Inchon secure on 16 September. That same day the EUSA began its break-out through the NKPA forces surrounding the Pusan Perimeter; an operation that lasted until 22 September. The EUSA's goals were to meet up with the X Corps while driving the remnants of the enemy before them.

The link-up between the EUSA vanguard and X Corps would take place on 26 September near the South Korean town of Osan. It was located 22 miles south of Seoul, and near the site where Task Force Smith had met its demise at the hands of the NKPA on 25 July.

Forward to Seoul

On the morning of 16 September, Marine Corsair pilots discovered six T-34-85 tanks lacking infantry support about 5 miles in front of the 5th Marine Regiment supported by tanks. The pilots radioed to the Marines that they had disposed of the enemy tanks using rockets and napalm. However, upon arriving on the scene, Marine tankers discovered that only two had been knocked out and three were left operational. What then transpired appears in the following passage from a USMC historical publication:

> Looking down from their vantage point, the tank crews saw three intact T-34s parked in column on the highway, about 300 yards beyond the turn. Hatches on the Communist vehicles were buttoned, with the 85mm guns leveled at the bend. The M26s opened up immediately. Twenty rounds of 90mm armor-piercing (AP) ammunition crashed into the enemy armor. There was no return

---

Table of Organization

The heart and soul of Marine Corps and US Army infantry divisions during the Second World War through to the Korean War were their three infantry regiments, besides the three infantry regiments of around 4,000 men each contributed by the 1st Marine Division for the Korean conflict. The US Army would eventually deploy twenty-six infantry regiments and the ROKA forty-two infantry regiments.

The Marine Corps infantry regiments as well as those of the US Army and the ROKA shared the same triangular structure, with each regiment subdivided into three infantry battalions of approximately 1,000 men each. The latter were further subdivided into three rifle companies of anywhere between 180 and 240 men. Colonels commanded regiments and lieutenant colonels battalions, while captains were responsible for companies.

---

fire, probably because the Red crews had not time to elevate and traverse their manually-operated guns. In the space of a few minutes, each of the T-34s exploded and burst into flame. The crews did not escape.

On the evening of 16 September, as the 5th Marine Regiment advanced in the direction of Seoul, they dug in for the night near Ascom City, a supply base built by the US Army Service Command before the North Korean invasion. The NKPA had assembled a counterattacking force of six tanks and approximately 200 infantrymen to stop the Marines. Unaware of how far the Marines had pushed forward, the enemy blundered into their defensive positions in the pre-dawn darkness of 17 September, at which point the Marines opened fire.

A Marine historian described the fighting that morning:

> The Red infantry went down under the hail of lead like wheat under the sickle. Soldiers on the tanks were knocked to the road, where many were ground under the big vehicles lurching and roaring crazily in reaction to the surprise … The T-34s didn't have a chance. All of them exploded under the heavy fusillade; and when the smoke cleared, they were heaps of burning wreckage.

Kimpo Airfield

A most sought-after prize as part of the Inchon landing and advance towards Seoul was the securing of Kimpo airfield. That occurred on the morning of 18 September after the 5th Marine Regiment repulsed some half-hearted attacks by the 500 or so North Koreans guarding the facility. The Marine ground units had taken great care during the fighting to preserve the airfield's infrastructure for use by their supporting Marine aviation units.

As soon as the airfield was secured, Marine helicopters began flying in. At the same time, engineers were making temporary repairs to bring the airfield up to full operational capacity. Based on the advice of senior Marine leaders at the airfield, the X Corps' commanding officer authorized the establishment of MAG-33 of the 1st MAW at Kimpo that same day.

Many of the combat aircraft of MAG-33 began to fly into Kimpo airfield on 19 September. Their presence at the airfield meant less in-transit flight time, faster response to calls for ground support and nearby touch-down for damaged aircraft. Some of the remaining MAG-33 combat aircraft continued to operate off US Navy aircraft carriers near Inchon.

Taken from a USMC historical publication a young Marine officer describes his first experience with a strike by Marine Corsairs on a nearby enemy defensive position:

> The first of the gull-winged, dark blue Corsairs peeled from the circle and dove at the white smoke. Red tracers from its guns poured from the forward edges

of the wings. The plane leveled off only yards above the ridgeline. We could see the pilot in the cockpit and the big, white Marine Corps emblem on the fuselage … Then the [next] plane came in, this one dropping a pod of napalm. The black, coffin-shaped canister hit the ground, skipped a few feet above the surface, and exploded into a wall of flame that extended the length of the North Koreans' position. Two hundred yards below, we felt the shock of its explosion and a wave of searing heat.

5th Marine Regiment Movements

Seoul was located on the eastern side of the Han River. The 5th Marine Regiment on the river's western side was ordered to check out a former ferry-crossing site located 8 miles north of Seoul on 19 September. Once inspected and finding it suitable for their purposes, they were to cross the 400-yard-wide river the next day. For that operation, the 5th Marine Regiment had an amphibian tractor battalion and a company of amphibious trucks nicknamed 'Ducks' (DUKWs).

Unfortunately, the first Marine company that attempted the river crossing in the morning darkness of 20 September was turned back by fire from an undetected NKPA unit. A USMC historical publication describes the 5th Marine Regiment's initial attempt to cross the river: 'Amphibian tractors were hardly stealthy vehicles. We received enemy fire as soon as the vehicles entered the water. You could hear machine-gun rounds plinking against the armored cab. Mortar rounds, possibly from our own "four-deuce" [4.2in mortar] tubes, were exploding in the river.'

Air support and targeted supporting ground fire preceded the 5th Marine Regiment's second attempt carried out in the morning light of 20 September. It was much better organized and thought out, and proved successful. Engineers ferried Marine tanks across the river using two pontoon rafts brought from the United States for just such a situation. Once on the eastern side of the river, the 5th Marine Regiment quickly expanded their position and by the afternoon of the 20th was halfway to Seoul.

The commander of the 5th Marine Regiment, however, remained worried about securing a string of enemy-defended hills on the north-western approaches to Seoul. He was reassured by MacArthur that 'They'll all evaporate very shortly.' That did not turn out to be true, as by the afternoon of 20 September enemy resistance quickly strengthened and the Marine advance came to an abrupt halt.

A Marine officer described the enemy fire from one of their hilltop positions:

[The hill] was no vacation spot. Before the sunset, enemy heavy machine guns began to scythe back and forth over the hilltop, while anti-tank guns, accurate as a sniper rifle and a lot deadlier, flash-banged in with high-velocity rounds that left no time for a man to duck.

One of the enemy's hilltop positions facing the advance of the 5th Marine Regiment received the nickname of 'Smith's Ridge' after a Marine company commander assigned its capture. Before the final Marine ground assault, NKPA positions underwent endless attacks by Marine artillery and air support.

Capturing Smith's Ridge did not come cheap. It cost one company of the 2nd Battalion, 5th Marine Regiment 178 casualties out of 206 men. The estimated enemy body count topped out at more than 1,500 dead. The officer after whom the ridge was named lost his life in the fighting.

A Marine officer that had observed the 2nd Battalion begin their assault on Smith's Ridge wrote an article in a 1956 issue of the *Marine Corps Gazette*. In that article, he recorded what he witnessed when the Marine riflemen reached the enemy lines on 23 September: '... yelling wildly and firing their rifles, carbines, and BARs [Browning Automatic Rifles]. They entered upon a scene of carnage stretching out in every direction. Driving forward through the human wreckage, they shot and bayoneted anything that moved.'

Despite the successful seizure of Smith's Ridge and others, there remained stiff fighting before the 5th Marine Regiment finally reached the hills overlooking Seoul on 25 September.

1st Marine Regiment Movements

On 18 September, the 1st Marine Regiment received orders to cross the Han River. However, before that could be accomplished, it had to capture the industrial city of Yeongdeungpo located on the western side of the Han River, opposite Seoul. To reach the city, the Marines had first to take a significant range of hills on the outskirts of the city, followed by crossing the Kalchon River.

On the night of 19 September, the 1st Marine Regiment was dug in outside of the small farming town of Sosa-ri. In the early-morning darkness of 20 September, the NKPA mounted another tank-led counterattack without knowing the Marines' positions. The enemy encountered a buzz-saw of Marine firepower.

From a USMC historical publication comes the following passage: 'Dawn of 20 September revealed a scene of utter ruin across the Marine front. The highway was littered with burnt NKPA trucks, tanks, and equipment. Heaped on the road, in ditches, and along hillsides were 300 enemy dead.'

By the end of the day on 20 September, the 1st Marine Regiment had captured their objective. An example of that day's fierce fighting appears in this extract from the Medal of Honor citation of First Lieutenant Henry A. Commiskey, 1st Marine Regiment:

Coolly disregarding the heavy enemy machine-gun and small-arms fire, he plunged on well forward of the rest of his platoon and was the first man to reach the crest of the objective. Armed only with a pistol, he jumped into a hostile machine-gun emplacement occupied by five enemy troops and quickly disposed of four of the soldiers with his automatic pistol. Grappling with the fifth, First Lieutenant Commiskey knocked him to the ground and held him until he could obtain a weapon from another member of his platoon and kill the last of the enemy gun crew. Continuing his bold assault, he moved to the next emplacement, killed two or more of the enemy and then led his platoon toward the rear nose of the hill to rout the remainder of the hostile troops and destroy them as they fled from their positions.

Taking Yeongdeungpo

The 1st Marine Regiment's assault on the city of Yeongdeungpo took place on 21 September against stiff enemy resistance. The commanding officer of an infantry battalion stated that fording the Kalchon River into the city was akin to crossing a medieval moat. He then went on to say that climbing over the numerous dikes that surrounded the city was like 'going over the top' in the trench fighting of the First World War. His battalion lost 217 men in crossing the Kalchon River to enter the city.

As fierce fighting raged on the outskirts of Yeongdeungpo on 21 September, a single company of the 1st Marine Regiment found an unprotected gap in the enemy's defensive line. The company then crossed the Kalchon River and proceeded through the centre of the city and out the other side unmolested. The company commander later remarked: 'It was eerie … we simply slithered into town undetected.' The Marine company quickly took up defensive positions on the far side of the city and remained unknown to the enemy until a formation of marching NKPA troops, singing political songs, blundered into them and were cut down.

On the night of 21 September, the Marine company on the far side of Yeongdeungpo prepared itself for the expected NKPA counterattack in the morning darkness of 22 September. Private First Class Morgan Brainard recalls the sounds and sights of enemy tanks as they approached:

> The squeaking and engine humming was drawing much closer, and as I crouched in my hole, I felt the ice-like shiver of pure fear. In the moonlight, I could see its turret with the long gun on it slowly circling back and forth, like some prehistoric, steel-backed monster sniffing for prey. I pressed tightly against the side of my hole, and waited for the flash and fire of its gun.

The five enemy tanks drove up and down a road facing the earthen dike behind which the Marine company had taken cover. They commenced firing their 85mm main guns, with little result as the soft ground of the embankment absorbed their explosive contents. The Marines, in turn, started firing 3.5in rocket-launchers at the enemy tanks, knocking out two and damaging another two.

Following the tanks were four enemy infantry assaults that were each repulsed by Marine firepower. With sunrise on 22 September, the Marines counted 210 enemy dead in front of their positions. Having lost heart, the enemy defenders of Yeongdeungpo withdrew as quickly as possible during the remainder of the day, allowing the 1st Marine Regiment to declare the city secure by the end of the day.

Into Seoul

The first elements of the 1st Marine Regiment crossed the Han River into the south-west suburbs of Seoul on 23 September. From a USMC historical publication: 'Now the rifle company assumed defensive positions on the objective, the men gazing in awe at the capital city arrayed to their north and east, sprawling virtually to the horizon.'

The commander of the 1st Marine Division was pleased that the 1st Marine Regiment had finally reached Seoul. On the other hand, he sensed the enemy's resistance was becoming tougher by the day, and the fighting quality of the opposing soldiers had much improved. The combat-inexperienced 7th Marine Regiment, which had arrived at Inchon on 21 September, was assigned the job of securing the high ground along a vital highway 6 miles north of Seoul's city centre on 25 September.

Preventing Collateral Damage

On 25 September 1950, the 1st Marine Division attack into the centre of Seoul commenced. A significant problem for the Marines in their effort to secure the city was the fact that it remained home to several hundred thousand South Korean civilians. While down from its pre-war high of almost 1 million people prior to the North Korean invasion, it had been the fifth-largest city in Asia.

The need to minimize civilian casualties in the battle for Seoul forced a rethink by the leadership of MAG-33, reflected by a Marine lieutenant colonel: 'Bombing by its very nature gave way to the more easily accurate techniques of rocketing and

---

Tank Issues

Insight on the part played by Marine armour between 15 and 23 September appears in this extract from a US Army Korean War report titled *Employment of Armor in Korea: The First Year*:

> The Marines were often deprived of tank support in this operation because of the heavily sewn [sic] land mines in the vicinity of INCHON and YONGDUNG-PO [Yeongdeungpo] which delayed the movement of tanks. In the first four days of the operation, 24 enemy tank kills were claimed. The majority of this number were accounted for by 2.36" and 3.5" rocket-launchers.

strafing ... I feel we became increasingly aware of the need to avoid what we now call collateral damage.'

In the Heart of the City

To defend Seoul, the estimated 20,000 NKPA troops improvised barricades at almost every major intersection. These typically consisted of sand-filled rice bags and rubble stacked nearly 8ft high and defended by a variety of machine guns, anti-tank guns and mines. The latter were often Russian-made, reflecting the NKPA's Soviet Army instruction in mine warfare tactics.

It took Marine ground units between forty-five and sixty minutes to clear individual barricades. The process began with a rifle company commander subjecting the enemy barricade and its defenders to as much firepower as could be mustered.

Under cover of smoke and white phosphorus rounds, Marine engineers would rush forward to clear the area around the barricades of mines. Then the tanks came in, followed by the infantry. Sometimes a tank would come in contact with an undiscovered mine. More often Marine engineers or infantrymen would be killed or wounded in the process of securing a barricade.

A Marine officer described taking on an enemy barricade: 'We had it hot and heavy among the burning buildings and the crumbled sandbags of the barricades, and then they broke and ran ... and we butchered them among the Russian AT [anti-tank] guns and the Japanese Nambu machine guns.'

As the Marines advanced towards the barricades, they were also under constant fire from enemy snipers. The Marine tanks had to run a gauntlet of NKPA troops lobbing Molotov cocktails from the roofs of buildings that lined the streets. In the middle of this chaos would be thousands of terrified South Koreans desperately trying to avoid the fighting, but instead being killed or wounded in the crossfire.

At one point in the battle for Seoul a Marine flame-thrower tank was attacked by a single enemy soldier, as is described below in a USMC historical publication:

> Ignoring the Marine infantrymen, who gaped in disbelief, the North Korean hurled a huge satchel charge over the engine compartment of the armored vehicle, then escaped unharmed as the explosion rocked the area. The flame tank was wrecked, but the crew escaped serious injury with the assistance of supporting infantry. Apparently, a suicide squad of NNKPA demolition men had been assigned the mission of destroying Marine armor in this fashion.

Once aware of the situation, Marine riflemen assigned to accompany Marine tanks were much more careful, and a hail of gunfire foiled subsequent attempts by individual enemy soldiers to duplicate the first tank attack.

From a USMC historical publication is an extract by Private First Class Morgan Brainard describing the fierceness and brutality involved in trying to clear buildings of enemy troops: 'The tension from these little forays whittled us pretty keen ... I think if one's own mother had suddenly leapt out in front of us, she would have been cut down immediately, and we all would probably have cheered with the break in the tension.'

A Funny Business

In the early evening of 25 September, a message came in from Lieutenant General Almond, the X Corps commander, to the 1st Marine Division command post. Claiming that the enemy was fleeing the city, the message directed the division: 'You will push attack now to the limits of your objectives in order to insure [*sic*] maximum destruction of enemy forces. Signed Almond.'

For the Marine officers, the X Corps order made little sense. One Marine company commander stated his main concerns: 'A night attack without reconnaissance or rehearsal? What are our objectives?' Nevertheless, the Marines of the 1st Division began pulling themselves together for the ordered advance.

Shortly before midnight on the 25th, the NKPA beat the Marines in Seoul to the punch with a counterattack by an armoured brigade. Such was the scale of the counterattack that the commanding officer of the 1st Marine Division quickly cancelled the planned nighttime attack. The NKPA units in Seoul also counter-attacked a US Army 7th Infantry Division RCT now within the city limits. NKPA losses from their failed nighttime counterattacks were estimated to number at least 500 men and a dozen or more armoured vehicles.

The next morning, 26 September, the men of the 1st Marine Division were surprised to hear of a communiqué issued the previous afternoon of the 25th by the X Corps commander. In that communiqué he stated: 'Three months to the day after the North Koreans launched their surprise attack south of the 38th Parallel the combat troops of the X Corps recaptured the capital city of Seoul. The enemy is fleeing the city to the north-east.' To no one's surprise, many wondered why the NKPA soldiers still in Seoul hadn't heard the good news.

Seoul is Secured

As events proved, the X Corps commander was partly correct; the NKPA main body had begun withdrawing from Seoul during the night of 25 September. The enemy armoured brigade had remained behind as a delaying force. It would take another forty-eight hours' fighting before the city was secure from organized enemy resistance on 27 September.

One Marine private described the damage to Seoul from the fighting: '... great gaping skeletons of blackened buildings with their windows blown out ... telephone wires hanging down loosely from their drunken, leaning poles; glass and bricks every-where; literally a town shot to hell.'

It was on 27 September that the Marines of the 1st and 5th Regiments finally joined up near the centre of Seoul. There then took place a good-natured race between the Marine regiments to see who could reach the city centre first and take down some large red banners flying over the former South Korean capital. That honour fell to the 5th Marine Regiment.

The Marines of the 1st and 5th Regiments also planted American flags on a great many other buildings in Seoul that day including the former Soviet embassy. One old Marine sergeant was quoted as saying: 'It looked like the 4th of July around here.'

Marine losses during the Inchon-Seoul campaign came out at 2,330 men with 364 killed, 1,961 wounded of whom 53 later died of their wounds, and 5 missing in action. The most significant single day's losses occurred on 24 September with casualties of 285 men. Enemy losses were put at more than 10,000 men with another 7,000 becoming PoWs.

In Pursuit of the Enemy

With Seoul secure, the X Corps' commanding officer ordered the reinforced 7th Marine Regiment to secure an important road junction 16 miles due north of Seoul known as Uijeongbu. That would take place between 1 and 3 October.

First the Marines would have to clear a section of highway that passed through a narrow defile. In the bloody fighting that occurred, a young Marine mortar officer remembered: 'The North Koreans used whistles and bugles for battlefield command, more effective by far than our walkie-talkies.'

On the morning of 3 October, the 7th Marine Regiment began punching through the enemy's defensive positions at the narrow defile and went on to capture Uijeongbu by the afternoon. In taking the road junction they had 13 killed and 111 wounded. On 3 October the Marines of the 1st Division were ordered to halt. Their sector was then assigned to the 1st Cavalry Division of the EUSA.

The Conquering Hero

MacArthur arrived in Seoul on 29 September, along with South Korean President Syngman Rhee. At noon in the National Assembly chamber, MacArthur made a formal pronouncement, as he was so fond of doing, to the South Korean president:

> By the grace of a merciful Providence, our forces fighting under the standard of that greatest hope and inspiration of mankind, the United Nations, have liberated this ancient capital city of Korea. On behalf of the United Nations Command, I am happy to restore to you, Mr. President, the seat of your government that from it you may better fulfil your constitutional responsibilities.

The South Korean president answered: 'How can I ever explain to you my own undying gratitude and that of the Korean people?'

Marines are seen here having the .30 calibre water-cooled M1917A1 machine gun explained to them. MacArthur badly wanted the 1st Marine Division for his amphibious invasion of Inchon, a port occupied by the North Koreans. This would be followed by the freeing of Seoul, the South Korean capital, from enemy control. MacArthur finally got his approval for the Marine division from the Joint Chiefs of Staff (JCS) on 25 July 1950. (*USMC*)

Marine Corps Major General Oliver P. Smith took command of the 1st Marine Division on 25 July 1950. Upon his arrival at Camp Pendleton, located in Southern California, the division had only 3,459 men out of a theoretical strength on paper of approximately 22,000 men. To bring the division to full strength, the Marines called up its reservists, which included a great many Second World War veterans. (*USMC*)

(**Above**) Pictured here during a training exercise are Marines posing with a .30 calibre M1919A4 air-cooled machine gun. The Marine Corps had two types of reservists: the 33,527 men of the 'Organized Reserve' that conducted both monthly drills and summer active duty, and the 'Volunteer Marine Corps' of 90,044 men and women, most of them veterans, who had not trained since leaving the Corps. (*USMC*)

(**Opposite, above**) By 7 August 1950, the 1st Marine Division was up to 17,681 men. Loading up the not yet fully manned Marine division for deployment to Japan was completed by 22 August 1950. The incomplete division sailed to Japan using nineteen commercial ships as the US Navy was short of transport ships. Here Marines conduct bayonet practice while on board ship. (*USMC*)

(**Opposite, below**) Between 5 and 12 September 1950, the still incomplete 1st Marine Division departed Japan from two different ports, planning to meet up outside the enemy-occupied port of Inchon, as seen on this map. Leaving the port of Pusan on 14 September 1950, the 1st Provisional Marine Brigade was to meet up with the 1st Marine Division outside of Inchon and be re-absorbed by the division, its parent unit. (*USMC*)

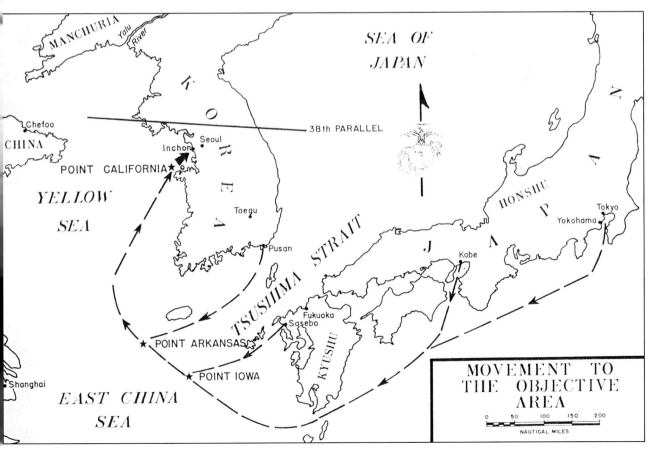

MOVEMENT TO
THE OBJECTIVE
AREA

An example of the six US Navy assault transports employed for the amphibious invasion of Inchon. Other vessels used included eight assault cargo transports. Even with the 1st Provisional Marine Brigade re-absorbed into the 1st Marine Division off the coast of Inchon, the division was still missing its third infantry regiment, the 7th. The 7th would not arrive at Inchon until 21 September 1950. (*USMC*)

Included in the Inchon invasion plans was the US Army 7th Infantry Division. To oversee the two-division invasion force, the US Army X Corps was activated in Japan on 26 August 1950. MacArthur appointed his chief of staff, Major General Edward M. Almond, to its command rather than the higher-ranking and more experienced Marine Lieutenant General Lemuel C. Shepherd Jr seen here on the right. (*US Navy*)

Pre-invasion aerial bombardment of Inchon by both Marine Corps and US Navy aircraft began on 10 September 1950. Pictured here are Marine F4U-4B Corsairs prepared for take-off from the flight deck of the Second World War-era US Navy aircraft carrier the *Badoeng Strait* (CVE-116) for an attack on enemy defensive positions in and around Inchon. (*USMC*)

An illustration of the planned amphibious assault on Inchon slated for 15 September, named Operation CHROMITE. Normally an endeavour of such proportions would have involved at least a couple of months of planning and training, but there had been no time for that. The main Marine landings would take place at Red Beach by the 5th Marine (Infantry) Regiment and Blue Beach by the 1st Marine (Infantry) Regiment.

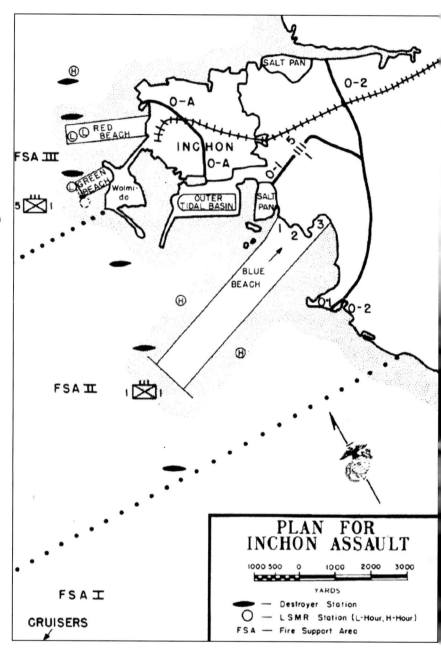

(**Opposite, above**) US Navy cruisers, including the USS *Rochester* (CA-124) seen here, began conducting the pre-landing bombardment of Inchon on the morning of 13 September. The cruisers belonged to Joint Task Force Seven, which totalled 230 ships including 5 US Navy aircraft carriers of various types. Other UN navies also contributed ships to the operation. (*US Navy*)

(**Opposite, below**) Dominating the entrance to Inchon was Wolmi-do Island, connected to the city by a causeway. It had to be secured before the two main landings at Inchon could take place. For this assignment, a battalion of Marines from the 5th Marine (Infantry) Regiment, supported by tanks, landed on the island on the morning of 15 September. Pictured here is a Marine using a flame-thrower to clear an enemy bunker. (*USMC*)

(**Above**) A Marine M4A3 medium tank armed with a 105mm howitzer is seen here during the fighting for Wolmi-do Island. In the foreground are enemy dead with others in the background having surrendered. The Marines encountered only half-hearted resistance in securing Wolmi-do and a much smaller nearby island connected to it by a causeway in the early-morning hours of 15 September. (USMC)

(**Opposite, above**) Taken during the pre-invasion bombardment of Inchon is this picture of the port city suffering from several out of control fires. The landing location for the 5th Marine (Infantry) Regiment would be in the lower right quadrant of the photograph labelled Beach Red. The 1st Marine (Infantry) Regiment would land at Beach Blue at the centre uppermost quadrant of the image. (USMC)

(**Opposite, below**) To land the 5th Marine (Infantry) Regiment at Red Beach, the US Navy employed a large number of LCVPs (Landing Craft Vehicle Personnel), an example of which is pictured here. More than 20,000 were manufactured during the Second World War. Powered by a single diesel engine, the vessel had a top speed of 14 mph and could carry as many as thirty-six troops. (US Navy)

Red Beach was, in reality, not a sandy beach; rather it consisted of a 15ft-high concrete and rock seawall as seen in this picture with an LCVP abutting up against it at high tide. At low tide there was no beach, only a wide mudflat. To assist the Marines in getting over the seawall at high tide, each LCVP was provided with two improvised wooden ladders equipped with scaling hooks. *(US Navy)*

From a seat on the US Navy command ship, the USS *Mount McKinley* (AGC-7), MacArthur is observing the Inchon landing. Also seen, from left to right, are US Navy Rear Admiral James H. Doyle, US Army Brigadier Edwin K. Wright (MacArthur's Operations Officer) and Major General Edward M. Almond, who MacArthur had appointed as the X Corps' commanding officer. *(US Army)*

In this classic image are Marines of the 5th (Infantry) Regiment having just reached the seawall at Red Beach on 15 September, having already raised their wooden scaling ladders. The lead Marine climbing out of the landing craft and over the seawall is First Lieutenant Baldomero Lopez, who moments later lost his life in destroying an enemy bunker to save his men, for which he received the Medal of Honor. (USMC)

(**Opposite, above**) The 1st Marine (Infantry) Regiment's landing zone, Beach Blue, 3 miles north of Beach Red, had no seawall, so the leading wave of vehicles consisted of US Army LVT(A)-4s (Landing Vehicle Tracked (Armoured) No. 4). Introduced into service in March 1944, the LVT(A)-4 had an open-topped armoured turret armed with a 75mm howitzer, as seen in this image. (*Pierre-Olivier Buan*)

(**Above**) Following the US Army LVT(A)-4s onto Beach Blue were two different versions of the Marine Corps LVT-3, with the original version pictured here introduced into service in 1945. A total of 2,962 units came off the assembly lines during the Second World War. LVT-3s were built unarmoured. However, add-on armour kits were added in the field. Armament consisted only of machine guns. (*Patton Museum*)

(**Opposite, below**) Also employed during the Inchon invasion was the LVT-3C seen here, a modernized version of the original LVT-3. Design improvements included raised sides along with the rear compartment as well as foldable aluminium overhead covers. It came with a small one-man machine-gun-equipped turret. A total of 1,200 modernized units of the LVT-3 series entered Marine service. (*Paul Hannah*)

14

(**Opposite, above**) Besides the various types of US Navy landing craft and US Army and Marine Corps LVTs that participated in the Inchon landing, there was also the 1st Amphibian Truck Company equipped with the 2.5-ton DUKW seen here, unofficially nicknamed 'the Duck'. Its primary job was to move artillery pieces and ammunition and other supplies. (*Pierre-Olivier Buan*)

(**Above**) Disembarking from a US Navy Landing Ship Tank (LST) is a Marine Corps M26 Pershing medium tank. Just before the 1st (Marine) Tank Battalion set sail to Japan in mid-August 1950, its M4A3 medium tanks were replaced with Pershing tanks. Hence the only training the crews received on their new vehicles prior to the Inchon landing was on board the LSTs. (*USMC*)

(**Opposite, below**) The port of Inchon has the world's second-highest tidal variations, averaging 28ft. To provide the US Navy's landing craft enough water under their hulls to mount the amphibious invasion, MacArthur had to land in either mid-September or mid-October. Seen here at Inchon during low tide are a stranded US Navy Landing Craft Medium (LCM) in the foreground and an LST in the background. (*US Navy*)

(**Above**) There was a great deal of confusion during the amphibious invasion of Inchon due to the haste with which it took place. Against a resolute and well-trained enemy force this could have resulted in heavy losses to the Marine Corps. However, as the enemy units defending Inchon were minimal and second-rate, Operation CHROMITE was a great success. Teenage enemy prisoners are seen in this picture, taken during the fighting for Inchon. (*USMC*)

(**Opposite, above**) In this map we see the Marines' progress on Day Two of the amphibious invasion of Inchon. Total Marine losses for the first day of Operation CHROMITE were 20 killed, 1 dead of wounds, 1 missing in action and 174 wounded. On Day Two the plans called for the 1st and 5th Marine (Infantry) regiments to form a line abreast for their advance to Seoul, located 20 miles east. (*USMC*)

(**Opposite, below**) The initial encounter with NKPA tanks by the 1st Marine Division during the advance on Seoul took place in the daylight hours of 16 September. The NKPA tanks were destroyed by a combination of Marine aircraft and tanks. On the nights of 16 and 17 September, enemy tanks supported by infantry unknowingly blundered into Marine defensive positions and suffered heavy losses. Pictured here is a destroyed T-34-85 medium tank. (*USMC*)

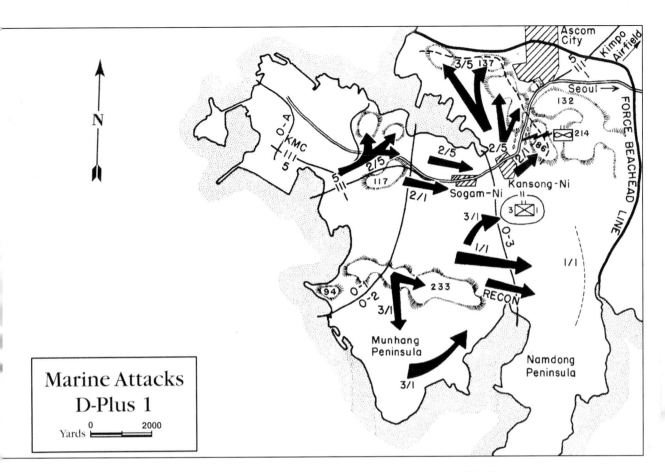

Marine Attacks
D-Plus 1

Yards 0 — 2000

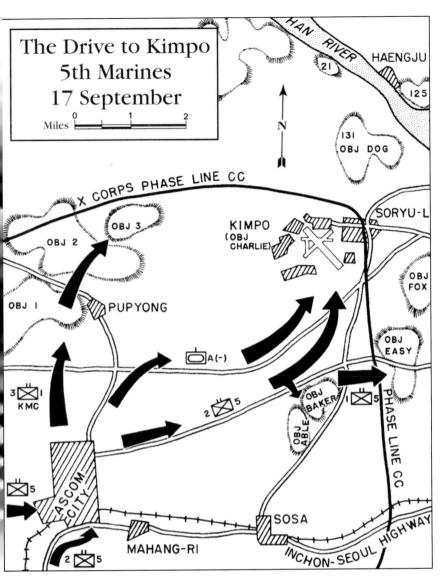

**The Drive to Kimpo
5th Marines
17 September**

Miles 0 1 2

N

HAN RIVER

HAENGJU

21

125

131
OBJ DOG

X CORPS PHASE LINE CC

OBJ 3

OBJ 2

KIMPO
(OBJ CHARLIE)

SORYU-L

OBJ FOX

OBJ 1

PUPYONG

A(-)

OBJ EASY

3 KMC

2 5

OBJ BAKER

1 5

OBJ ABLE

PHASE LINE CC

5

ASCOM CITY

SOSA

INCHON-SEOUL HIGHWAY

MAHANG-RI

2 5

The map shows the advance of the 5th Marine infantry Regiment as it approached Kimpo airfield, the finest in South Korea prior to the war. At the top of the map is the Han River, the regiment's next goal after securing the airfield. Visible at the bottom of the map is the Inchon-Seoul Highway with the adjoining railroad. The area labelled ASCOM City had been a US Army logistic site from 1945 until 1948. (*USMC*)

(**Opposite, above**) Marines of the 1st Division are hitching rides on a tank and LVT-3s in the background as they advance towards Seoul. With only two of its three infantry regiments present, the 1st Marine Division used the Inchon-Seoul Highway that ran from west to east as a dividing line, with the 5th Marine (Infantry) Regiment advancing on the northern side of the highway (and adjoining railroad tracks) and the 1st Marine (Infantry) Regiment on the southern side. (*USMC*)

(**Opposite, below**) In a burned-out hangar at Kimpo airfield is a fairly complete Soviet-built IL-2 Sturmovik ground-attack aircraft of Second World War vintage. The Soviet Union had supplied the North Korean Air Force (NKAF) with around 180 prop-driven aircraft prior to the start of the Korean War. The American Fifth Air Force and US Navy aerial assets destroyed the majority of the NKAF's aircraft by mid-July 1950. (*USMC*)

(**Above**) Among the armoured vehicles provided to the NKPA before the Korean War was the BA-64 armoured car pictured here. The vehicle had a crew of two and had a small open-topped turret armed with a machine gun. Designed as a reconnaissance vehicle for the Red Army during the Second World War, it performed the same role for NKPA tank units. (*Pierre-Olivier Buan*)

(**Opposite, above**) US Army LVT(A)-4s and Marine Corps LVT-3Cs are shown crossing the Han River at a location north of Seoul on 20 September. The first attempt by the 5th Marine (Infantry) Regiment in crossing the river proved unsuccessful due to a nearby enemy unit that had not been spotted. The second attempt was preceded by heavy aerial and artillery support and proved successful. (*USMC*)

(**Opposite, below**) American Marines and South Korean Marines are shown in the personnel/cargo compartment of an LVT-3C in the process of being ferried across the Han River. The vehicle's rear compartment had a hinged rear ramp and sufficient space to accommodate a single Jeep or a 105mm towed howitzer. Power was supplied by two gasoline engines. (*USMC*)

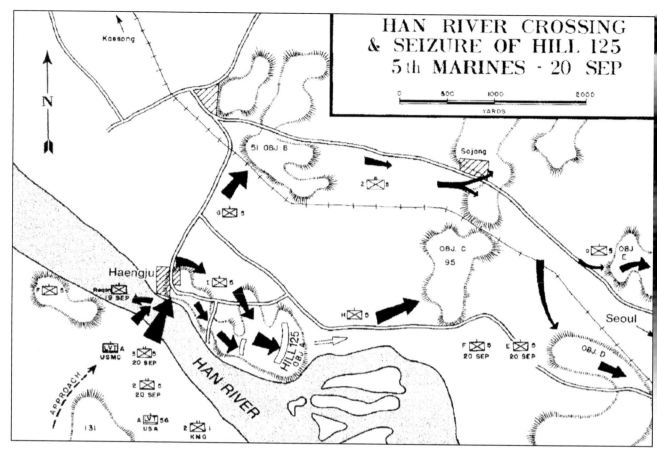

HAN RIVER CROSSING
& SEIZURE OF HILL 125
5th MARINES · 20 SEP

0   500   1000   2000
YARDS

Kaesong

Sojong

51 OBJ B

2 ☒ 5

G ☒ 5

OBJ. C
95

D ☒ 5

OBJ
E

Haengju

Regt
19 SEP

F ☒ 5

I ☒ 5

HILL 125
OBJ. A

H ☒ 5

Seoul

OBJ. D

A ☒ USMC
20 SEP

3 ☒ 5
20 SEP

F ☒ 5
20 SEP

E ☒ 5
20 SEP

APPROACH

2 ☒ 5
20 SEP

131

A ☒ 56
USA

2 ☒ 1
KMC

HAN RIVER

(**Opposite, above**) Once on the opposite side of the Han River, the 5th Marine (Infantry) Regiment headed south towards Seoul. However, they quickly encountered stiff enemy resistance along a string of ridges that blocked that path as seen in this map. The Marine regimental commander had anticipated such a development, but had been reassured by MacArthur that it would not be the case. (*USMC*)

(**Above**) A Marine tanker poses in front of his M26 Pershing medium tank. Behind his shoulder painted on the ventilation hump located between the driver and assistant driver's positions are the outlines of three tanks that he and the crew had accounted for in battle. Those who crewed the Pershing tanks appreciated their thick frontal armour and powerful 90mm main gun. What they did not care for were the 500hp gasoline engines that proved underpowered for the tank's weight. (*USMC*)

(**Opposite, below**) To protect the northern approaches to Seoul from the advance of the 5th Marine (Infantry) Regiment the NKPA amassed a force of approximately 10,000 men. The enemy soldiers lacked combat experience but made up for it for by being both well-trained and well-led. The machine-gun platoon of a Marine rifle company during the Korean War had six .30 calibre M1919A4 machine guns as pictured here. (*USMC*)

The NKPA received the complete line of Red Army mortars employed during the Second World War, including the M37 82mm mortar pictured here. It could fire an approximately 6lb projectile out to a range of 3,200 yards. In addition, the NKPA was supplied with Red Army 60mm and 120mm mortars. *(Vladimir Yakubov)*

(**Opposite, above**) In their advance to Seoul the 5th Marine (Infantry) Regiment found itself outnumbered, but this was offset by their on-call aerial support which the NKPA learned to greatly fear. Marine ground crewmen are seen here manhandling a cart full of rockets towards the F4U-4B Corsairs in the background. During the hours of darkness the 11th Marine (Artillery) Regiment filled in for the fire-support role. *(USMC)*

(**Opposite, below**) On the same day (20 September) that the 5th Marine (Infantry) Regiment crossed the Han River north of Seoul, the 1st Marine (Infantry) Regiment commenced its main attack on the industrial city of Yeongdeungpo on the west side of the Han River directly across from Seoul as seen on this map. The X Corps' commander, Major General Almond, gave permission for the burning down of the city to aid in its capture. *(USMC)*

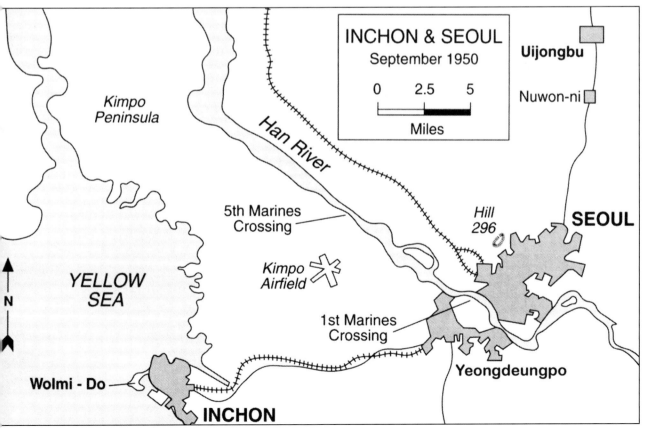

With the reactivation of the 1st Marine (Infantry) Regiment on 4 August, as part of the 1st Marine Division, command was assigned to Colonel Lewis B. 'Chesty' Puller, a much-decorated member of the corps known for his 'lead from the front' attitude. By August 1950, he had been awarded four US Navy Crosses for his personal bravery and leadership in battle. (*USMC*)

Marines are shown here guarding enemy prisoners. The 1st Marine (Infantry) Regiment managed to secure Yeongdeungpo by the end of the day, 22 September, after fierce fighting including tank-led attacks. The following day, Colonel Puller's regiment successfully crossed the Han River into Seoul, with the 5th Marine (Infantry) Regiment providing covering fire. (*USMC*)

An M26 Pershing tank of the 5th Marine Regiment is shown here in Seoul. These tanks provided a crucial edge to the 1st Marine Division fighting in Seoul and would account for thirteen enemy tanks and fifty-six anti-tank guns by the time the city was secured. In the process the Marine 1st Tank Battalion lost five Pershing tanks and two M4 series tanks. (*USMC*)

Having experienced over and over again the effectiveness of the Corsairs flown by both Marine Corps and US Navy pilots, the NKPA established a number of anti-aircraft positions in the city. Among the anti-aircraft guns supplied to the North Koreans was the 85mm Model 1943 pictured here. As had the Red Army in the Second World War, the NKPA also used it as an anti-tank gun. (*Vladimir Yakubov*)

(**Above**) Marines are shown here engaging the enemy in Seoul. The two Marines in the foreground are armed with M2 carbines and the Marine in the background an M1 rifle best known as the Garand. Not trained in street fighting, the Marines found themselves tasked with the capture of an enormous and sprawling city dominated by steep hills, defended by 20,000 enemy soldiers. (USMC)

(**Opposite, above**) Among the many types of machine guns supplied to the NKPA by the Soviet Union was the DShK 1938 pictured here. The 12.7mm machine gun, with armoured shield fitted, weighed in at approximately 346lb, hence the wheeled carriage also seen on other Red Army machine guns intended for infantry use. The gas-operated, air-cooled weapon had a rate of fire of around 600 rounds per minute. (Vladimir Yakubov)

(**Opposite, below**) One of the weapons that proved extremely helpful in the Marines' battle for Seoul was the 3.5in 'Super Bazooka' pictured here. One Marine is quoted as saying: 'We employed it in a very effective manner in Yongdungpo and in Seoul in the destruction of houses that had enemy in them. In many instances our 3.5 gunners simply shot at some of these fragile houses killing all the occupants.' (USMC)

(**Above**) Marines fighting in Seoul are shown warily scanning their surroundings for any sign of the enemy. Making matters even more difficult for the Marines was the fact that Seoul remained home to untold thousands of terrified refugees. This forced the battle-weary Marines to ensure target identification and limit indiscriminate firing. (*USMC*)

(**Opposite, above**) Throughout the Korean War the NKPA used civilian clothing to disguise their reconnaissance personnel. Sometimes groups of refugees would be herded in front of attacking enemy units to hide their presence until the last moment. Pictured here are Koreans crying over the bodies of their loved ones. (*USMC*)

(**Opposite, below**) When the 1st Marine Tank Battalion disembarked from their ships at Inchon they brought with them nine units of an M4 series medium tank armed with a flame-thrower and a 105mm howitzer. Developed during the last year of the Second World War, these were labelled the POA-CWS-H5 with an example pictured here in July 1945. They proved very useful, both in Seoul and in subsequent battles. (*Patton Museum*)

In this artwork we see a Marine forward artillery observer team during the fighting in Seoul. The 11th Marine (Artillery) Regiment had four artillery battalions. Three were armed with the M101 105mm howitzer. The fourth was armed with the M114 155mm howitzer which had a rate of fire of four rounds per minute and a range of 16,000 yards. (*USMC*)

(**Opposite, above**) Marines are shown here having flushed out a North Korean soldier from his sidewalk fighting position in Seoul. To force the enemy soldiers from their numerous defensive positions in the city required a great deal of teamwork among Marine engineers, tankers and infantrymen, including scout/snipers. Once an area was cleared, some Marines had to be left behind to prevent the enemy from returning. (*USMC*)

(**Opposite, below**) From an American military manual is this passage concerning how to begin a limited attack in an enemy-occupied city: 'The first phase of the attack should be conducted when visibility is poor. Troops should exploit poor visibility to cross open areas, to gain access to rooftops, to infiltrate enemy areas, and to gain a foothold. If the attack must be made when visibility is good, units should use smoke to conceal movement.' (*USMC*)

351390

(**Above**) On 26 September, a US Army unit from the EUSA met up with a US Army unit from MacArthur's X Corps advancing from Inchon. This marked one of MacArthur's key objectives for the Inchon invasion, to cut the NKPA supply lines to their forces around the Pusan Perimeter, allowing the EUSA to break out of its confinement. Pictured here are US Army M4A3(76)W medium tanks riding on the HVSS. (*Patton Museum*)

(**Opposite, above**) A Marine stretcher team is shown here in Seoul bringing a wounded comrade to a nearby aid station. Marine casualties during stiff fighting in Seoul from 25 to 27 September amounted to approximately 700 men. The combined Inchon-Seoul campaign cost the 1st Marine Division 2,450 casualties, with 415 killed or died of wounds, 2,029 wounded and 6 missing in action. (*USMC*)

(**Opposite, below**) Pictured during the fighting for Seoul is a Marine scout/sniper armed with an M1C Garand sniper rifle fitted with a commercially-designed and built telescope assigned the designation M82. Production of the M1C began in late 1944, but none saw action during the Second World War. A total of 8,000 examples of the M1C were manufactured. (*USMC*)

35/385

(**Above**) When Marines entered the former US consulate at Seoul to replace the North Korean flag flying above it with an American flag, they discovered the remains of the original Stars and Stripes that flew over the building in the trash at the rear of the consulate as seen in this photograph. On the left of the image is a Marine Corps sergeant and, on the right, an armed US Navy corpsman. (*USMC*)

(**Opposite, above**) As the NKPA forces in Seoul attempted to flee the city to the north, the X Corps' commander ordered the 1st Marine Division to seize and defend a series of blocking positions. That operation included the 5th Marine (Infantry) Regiment with the main effort falling to the 7th Marine (Infantry) Regiment. An M26 Pershing tank provides overwatch protection for advancing Marines. (*USMC*)

(**Opposite, below**) To assist the 7th Marine (Infantry) Regiment in its mission to cut off the NKPA's escape route from Seoul, the 1st Marine Division's commander assigned it a number of supporting units. These included a US Army anti-aircraft battery. Pictured here is a US Army M16A1 anti-aircraft half-track armed with four .50 calibre machine guns typically employed as an anti-personnel weapon during the Korean War. (*TACOM*)

Among the artillery pieces provided to the NKPA by the Soviet Union was the 76mm Regimental Gun Model 1927 shown here. Soviet factories built around 16,500 units of the weapon between 1928 and 1943. It fired a 13lb round out to a distance of 4,576 yards (2.6 miles). The weapon would be superseded by the 76mm Divisional Gun M1942 (ZiS-3) that had superior anti-tank performance. (*Vladimir Yakubov*)

Pictured here is the 76mm Divisional Gun M1942 (ZiS-3). Like all Red Army artillery pieces, it did double duty as an anti-tank gun. During the Second World War Soviet factories built approximately 100,000 units of the weapon. It fired an approximately 13lb high-explosive (HE) round to a maximum of around 14,000 yards (8 miles). (*Pierre-Olivier Buan*)

The principal air support for the 7th Marine (Infantry) Regiment in its efforts to cut off NKPA forces escaping from Seoul between 28 September and 3 October would be the Marine Squadron VMF-312, known as the 'Checkerboard squadron' from the paint scheme seen here on the engine cowling of one of their planes. (*USMC*)

Besides Corsairs, the 1st Marine Air Group (1st MAG) oversaw Marine transport squadrons that flew the civilian-designed, four-engine Douglas DC-4 as seen here being unloaded in Korea. In USAF service the aircraft was designated the C-54 Skymaster. With the Marine Corps the same plane received US Navy designation R5D-2. (*USMC*)

Chapter Three

Pushing Too Far

With X Corps' 26 September 1950 announcement of Seoul's capture and the link-up between it and the EUSA on the same day, there arose an American consensus that an opportunity had arisen to advance deep into North Korea. The American dream of a unified Western-facing Korea, under President Syngman Rhee, seemed within reach. President Truman authorized MacArthur to commence military operations north of the 38th Parallel on 27 September.

The JCS, worried about the expansion of the war, sent a message to MacArthur on 27 September authorizing him to proceed north of the 38th Parallel with some major restrictions. Only the ROKA could be used in those areas bordering on the Soviet Union or Red China. There could be no attacks on either country's territory, including naval or aircraft. If either Red Chinese or Soviet forces entered North Korea, only the ROKA could be employed north of the 38th Parallel.

It took the UN until 7 October to pass a vague resolution supporting Truman's decision. Previously, the UN had only sought that their forces drive NKPA forces north of the 38th Parallel, their fear being that a crossing of the 38th Parallel into North Korea by UN forces might cause Red Chinese or Soviet intervention.

Events Continue to Unfold

On 30 September, a ROKA division crossed the 38th Parallel into North Korea, joined by two more ROKA divisions between 6 and 7 October. President Syngman Rhee clearly stated on 19 September that no matter what President Truman or the UN decided regarding North Korea, 'we will not allow ourselves to stop.'

As American plans appeared for the invasion of North Korea, MacArthur issued the first of two surrender orders to the North Korean government on 1 and 9 October. In reality, nobody thought that the North Koreans would surrender, which they did not. The first American force to enter North Korea would be the 1st Cavalry Division of the EUSA on 9 October.

Red China Expresses Concern

American senior leadership gave little thought to how their Red Chinese counterparts would respond to the presence of a large hostile military force near their border. Red China issued many warnings, beginning on 20 August, that they would not tolerate an American-supported government on their border with North Korea. Their numerous warnings were seen only as bluffs to keep UN forces away from the border.

The Soviet representative to the UN also warned on 22 August about the possible widening of the conflict. It had become evident to the senior leadership of the Soviet Union and Red China that the North Korean invasion of South Korea had failed. They therefore correctly deduced that MacArthur's UN forces' command would advance into North Korea.

Red Chinese Premier Mao Tse-tung decided to intervene on behalf of the North Korean government on 4 October. Large numbers of Red Chinese Army formations, referred to by Western commentators as the Chinese Communist Force (CCF), began to enter North Korea between 14 and 20 October. By 20 October there were four CCF field armies in North Korea totalling approximately 130,000 men. The Red Chinese government referred to their soldiers entering North Korea as 'volunteers'.

Intelligence Failure

America's intelligence services missed the CCF movement into North Korea. As seen in a declassified CIA report dated 12 October 1950: 'Despite statements by Chou-En-Lai, troop movements to Manchuria, and propaganda charges of atrocities and border violations … there are no convincing indications of an actual Chinese Communist intention to resort to full-scale intervention in Korea' and 'such action is not probable in 1950'.

During a 15 October meeting with MacArthur, President Truman asked if he had any concerns about Red Chinese or Soviet military intervention. MacArthur's answer was 'very little'. He went on to say that if the Red Chinese did become involved, '… there would be the greatest slaughter' of their forces.

MacArthur thought little of the Chinese fighting man, having once commented that the Red Chinese military forces were 'grossly overrated'. He was convinced that US air power could quickly dispose of Red Chinese ground forces if encountered.

An Even Bigger Mistake

Surprisingly, the JCS had not thought much about what to do if the Inchon landing proved successful. Many have suggested that X Corps should have bypassed Seoul and advanced eastward across the Korean Peninsula. By doing so, they could block the KPA forces' retreat from the Pusan Perimeter in the face of the advancing EUSA.

Originally X Corps, which included the 1st Marine Division and the US Army 7th Infantry Division, was to be merged into the EUSA. However, MacArthur, wanting a striking force of his own with no regard for what the JCS or the White House wanted, kept X Corps separate from the EUSA.

In a passage from his book *The Coldest Winter: America and the Korean War*, author David Halberstam commented on MacArthur splitting the command of his ground forces:

> Of all the unspoken rules in the doctrine of the American Army, this was perhaps the most sacrosanct. It was something that you just did not do. When American military men thought of split commands, they thought immediately of the annihilation of George Armstrong Custer's forces at Little Big Horn.

MacArthur's Great Misadventure

On 3 October the 1st Marine Division began returning to Inchon, re-boarding ships in a process that continued until 15 October. The reason: MacArthur had decided to conduct another major amphibious assault, this time at the North Korean port city of Wonsan on the eastern side of the Korean Peninsula. His original plans had called for the landing to take place on 15 October, but that and many other deadlines quickly fell by the wayside.

The US Navy thought it made more sense and would be quicker if X Corps conducted a road march that would take it over the mountain highway that crossed the 38th Parallel, connecting Seoul on the west side of South Korea to Wonsan on the east side of North Korea. Rear Admiral Arleigh A. Burke, Deputy Chief of Staff to Commander Naval Forces Far East, stated:

> As events had developed, we objected to an amphibious assault as being unnecessary, it would take a lot of troops out of action for a long time when the enemy was already on the run. We felt that the same objective – to seize the port of Wonsan – could be achieved by marching the Tenth Corps up the road leading from Seoul to Wonsan.

MacArthur later claimed that nobody from the US Navy ever informed him of their objections.

In a US Army report dated May 1952 is a description of the highway that connected Seoul to Wonsan: 'This route is the best coast to coast route in Korea ... The Japanese designed and constructed this road ... the North Korean Government with Russian aid converted this highway into a first-class route. It is capable of supporting most types of traffic and is an all-weather route.'

The 1st Marine Division's leadership wondered if the landing was even needed, given the ROKA's successful advance up Korea's east coast. The Marines thought that the ROKA might secure the port city before a landing could even take place. They were correct: ROKA troops took Wonsan on 10 October.

Rather than re-boarding ships at Inchon which proved too crowded, the US Army 7th Infantry Division conducted a road march from Seoul south to Pusan. Once they arrived, they would load onto ships for their part in the upcoming amphibious operation. It took the division from 14 to 17 October to reach Pusan.

The Reason for the Wonsan Landing

On landing at Wonsan, X Corps was to push inland to the north-west quickly and capture the enemy capital of Pyongyang. By doing so, they would trap NKPA units between themselves and the EUSA advancing north along the Korean Peninsula's west coast.

In a USMC historical publication appears this passage: 'Almond's [the X Corps commander's] overriding ambition was to beat his rival, General Walker [of the EUSA], to the Yalu [the river that acted as the dividing line before North Korea and China].' Almond had under his command the 1st Marine Division and the US Army 7th Infantry Division, two ROKA divisions, and the US Army 3rd Infantry Division en route. The latter arrived at Wonsan between 5 and 17 November, bringing his total personnel to approximately 100,000 men.

Unexpected Hold-ups

The US Navy determined that the North Koreans should learn from their loss of Inchon. In the approaches to Wonsan, the North Koreans had sown more than 2,000 anti-shipping mines, both contact and magnetic. Making matters even worse, the US Navy had decommissioned all but twelve of its Second World War mine-sweepers. Two of the twelve struck mines on 12 October and sank. Even when reinforced with Japanese and South Korean craft, clearing the minefields proved overwhelming.

In the meantime, waiting for the minesweepers to clear a path, the transport ships carrying the 1st Marine Division remained at sea, reversing course every twelve hours. On board the crowded transports, Marines began referring to what they endured as 'Operation Yo-Yo'. A Marine historian voiced the complaint that 'Never did time die a harder death, and never did the grumblers have so much to grouse about.'

X Corps Finally Lands

The Marines were finally able to disembark at Wonsan between 26 and 28 October. From a USMC historical publication is the following passage on lessons learned:

> Inchon and Wonsan serve as book-end examples of amphibious warfare's risks and rewards … Wonsan, scheduled for attack by a larger and, by now, more experienced landing force against a sharply diminished enemy threat, should have been a snap. But in the irony of war, Inchon stands as a masterpiece, Wonsan as a laughing stock, as ill-conceived a landing as the United States ever conducted.

Rather than land at Wonsan, the US Army 7th Infantry Division was redirected to land on October 29th at the town of Iwon, already secured by the ROKA. It was located on the eastern side of the peninsula approximately 100 miles north of Wonsan. It took until 8 November before the entire division was ashore.

New Mission

The EUSA foiled MacArthur's plan for X Corps to seize the North Korean capital of Pyongyang by capturing the city on 19 October. New orders for the 1st Marine Division arrived for the division's commanding officer on 27 October. The division was to head approximately 50 miles north along Korea's east coast to the North Korean port of Hungnam, located halfway between Wonsan and the 7th Infantry Division, landing at Iwon.

Once the Marines reached Hungnam, they were to advance north-west, then to pass through the North Korean inland city of Hamhung and secure the eastern side of the Chosin Reservoir located around 50 miles from Hungnam. The port of Hungnam was cleared of sea mines by mid-November 1950.

Upon securing the Chosin Reservoir, the 1st Marine Division was to continue in a north-west direction to meet up with the EUSA at a selected phase line that only the ROKA could cross. On 24 November MacArthur dropped the phase line restriction on American military forces, allowing them to advance all the way to the Yalu River, the border between North Korea and Red China.

The 1st Marine Division commander proved so worried about X Corps' plans regarding his division that he penned a letter on 13 November to the commandant of the Marine Corps. In that letter, he explained that his division should not advance until the EUSA began its offensive on 24 November. He feared that his division would have its flanks unprotected if the EUSA advance did not go off as planned.

There was a 75- to 100-mile gap between the EUSA on the western side of the Korean Peninsula and the X Corps on the eastern side of the Korean Peninsula. In between these UN forces was the mountainous spine of the peninsula. Thought impassable by the American senior military leadership, the CCF managed to mass two army groups in that middle ground without being detected.

The Red Chinese Army Appears

On 25 October soldiers from the EUSA captured their first Red Chinese Army soldiers. That same day the CCF launched its initial advance against the ROKA 1st Division belonging to the EUSA. Historians describe it as the CCF's 'first phase offensive'. In the next week or so of fighting, the CCF would severely maul the ROKA 1st Division and others, including the US Army units assigned to reinforce them.

The commander of the EUSA quickly recalled his most forward units and began consolidating his forces along the Chongchon River. On 6 November the CCF disengaged, despite its overwhelming successes. Historians believe that the Red Chinese senior leadership was warning MacArthur not to cross the Chongchon River with his EUSA lest the CCF attack them once again.

Marines Encounter the CCF

On the eastern side of the Korean Peninsula, ROKA soldiers belonging to X Corps captured a small number of CCF soldiers on 25 October. The prisoners informed their captors of a large number of their fellow soldiers in the area, but none appeared.

On 1 November the leading element of the 1st Marine Division began moving from the inland North Korean town of Hamhung to the Chosin Reservoir. On the way, they encountered stiff resistance from a CCF division of around 8,000 men between 2 and 4 November 1950. The CCF division disengaged on 4 November with both sides having suffered heavy casualties.

Characteristic of the fighting is an extract from the 4 November action described in Medal of Honor recipient Sergeant James I. Poynter's citation:

> With his ranks critically depleted by casualties and he himself critically wounded as the [enemy] onslaught gained momentum and the hostile force surrounded his position, he seized his bayonet and engaged in bitter hand-to-hand combat as the breakthrough continued. Observing three machine guns closing in at a distance of 25 yards, he dashed from his position and, grasping hand grenades from fallen Marines as he ran, charged the emplacements in rapid succession, killing the crews of two and putting the other out of action before he fell, mortally wounded.

The Consequences of Ignoring a Warning

In spite of the CCF attacks against the EUSA and X Corps between 25 October and 7 November, American government and military officials failed to comprehend the significance of the CCF attacks and withdrawal. Those who voiced concern found themselves ignored. Most continued to believe that the CCF forces in North Korea were not a serious threat and that the UN ground forces should advance once more in spite of the arrival of winter.

On 24 November EUSA units on the south side of the Chongchon River crossed the river and launched a major offensive to secure the remainder of North Korea. The common belief at the time was that the Korean conflict would be over by Christmas of 1950. MacArthur even ordered ammunition resupply ships on the way to Korea to be diverted to Hawaii or turn around and return to the United States.

On the evening of 25 November, the CCF struck once again at the EUSA. The ground forces of the latter disintegrated and fled in an embarrassing rout. Historians label it as the CCF 'second phase offensive'. The US Army 2nd Infantry Division suffered more than 5,000 casualties and lost almost all of its artillery in the process. Compounding the EUSA's difficulties were more than 700,000 North Korean civilians who also fled south across the Chongchon River in the face of the CCF advance.

On 29 November the commander of the EUSA ordered a general withdrawal to new defensive lines near the North Korean capital of Pyongyang. The EUSA abandoned those defensive lines on 3 December and the city fell to the CCF on 5 December. The EUSA abandoned Seoul on 4 January 1951. Evacuation of Inchon began on 7 December 1950 and continued until 5 January 1951.

X Corps' Response

On 25 November the X Corps commander ordered a general offensive to begin on the morning of 27 November, in what has been called by one historian 'the most ill-advised and unfortunate operation of the Korean War.' The purpose was to relieve pressure on the EUSA located on the western side of the Korean Peninsula in the face of the overwhelming CCF advance.

The 1st Marine Division reached the southern tip of the Chosin Reservoir on 16 November. On 24 November the commander of the 1st Marine Division ordered the 5th and 7th Marine regiments up the western side of the Chosin Reservoir to the North Korean village of Yudam-ni. The 1st Marine Regiment would be based at the village of Koto-ri to guard the single supply line that reached back to Hungnam.

At that point, the 1st Marine Division had about 15,000 of its approximately 22,000 men near the Chosin Reservoir. The US Army 7th Infantry Division also had elements on the western side of the reservoir. The 1st Marine Division's head-quarters sat at the southern base of the reservoir at a location referred to as Hagaru-ri at which a crude airfield would be built. There was also an airfield built at Koto-ri.

They're Here!!!

On 26 November the Marines captured several Red Chinese soldiers who stated that there were three CCF divisions nearby. In truth, there were twelve CCF divisions in the general area with a total of around 150,000 men. Their goal, as part of the CCF second phase offensive, was the destruction of the 1st Marine Division.

The CCF attacked the Marines on the evening of 27 November. Even before that took place, the 1st Division Marines faced another enemy, 'the cold', as is recounted in the following extract from a USMC historical publication:

On Northwest Ridge, the infantrymen of 3/7 and 2/5 slowly grew numb from the penetrating cold. Trigger fingers, though heavily gloved, ached against the brittle steel of weapons, and parka hoods became encrusted with frozen moisture. In the cumbersome shoe-pacs, perspiration-soaked feet gradually became transformed into lumps of biting pain.

In relentless attacks against the 1st Marine Division regiments near the Chosin Reservoir and further south, the CCF suffered hefty losses. According to a USMC historical publication, '… grotesque heaps (of CCF soldiers) up and down the front'.

Small-Arms Experience in Korea

From a wartime report by US Army historian S.L.A. Marshall are comments on the crew-served weapons and small arms employed by the US Army and the USMC:

When temperatures shift from the sub-freezing to the sub-zero range, the greatest fluctuation in relative operating efficiency occurs among the mortars. When the ground becomes so hard that it is without cushioning effect, there is excessive buckling and cracking of base plates (under heavy firing) and firing pins break frequently. The whole family suffers damage, though the breakage rate is greatest in the 60mms [mortars]. The machine guns become more difficult in extreme cold because of heavy frost forming on the unjacketed parts; there is increased recourse to periodic warm-up firing to be sure of operation.

The BAR seems to stand up about as well under sub-zero as in sub-freezing conditions; there will be incidence of frost-lock in either situation. (Some BAR men cured this difficulty by urinating on their pieces.) However, the greater part of the trouble experienced in Korean operations with the BAR could not be blamed on temperature changes.

The M1 rifle works equally well in bitter or moderate cold. In fact, it is the 'old reliable' of infantry fighting during winter operations, and is not less dependable in other seasons. There are occasional mechanical failures for one reason or another. But outside of an occasional broken firing pin, the rifle structurally stands the cold phenomenally well. Frost will sometimes lock the piece if the man is careless about checking it. The ejector will fail if the chamber is excessively dirty; misfires will occur for the same reason. But the incidence of failure is relatively light and appears to be unrelated to major changes in temperature.

Despite their losses, the CCF managed to cut off and surround the 5th and 7th Marine regiments located in and around the village of Yudam-ni.

The fighting to repulse CCF attacks near the Chosin Reservoir appears in an extract from the Medal of Honor citation of Private Hector A. Cafferata Jr:

> Making a target of himself under the devastating fire from automatic weapons, rifles, grenades and mortars, he maneuvered up and down the line and delivered accurate and effective fire against the onrushing force, killing fifteen, wounding many more, and forcing the others to withdraw so that reinforcements could move up and consolidate the position.

On 28 November, MacArthur finally concluded that the CCF offensive against X Corps and the EUSA was much more severe than he had thought. MacArthur ordered that all offensive actions halt and that everyone was to go on the defensive. The X Corps commander issued an order on 30 November that all the corps' divisions withdraw to the port of Hungnam in the face of the CCF offensive.

To restore the road connection between the 1st Marine Division headquarters, located at Hagaru-ri south of the reservoir, 'Task Force Drysdale', composed of Marine tanks, British Royal Marines and elements of the US Army 7th Infantry Division, attempted to break through CCF roadblocks on 29 November without success and endured heavy losses in the attempt.

The Marine Break-out

On 30 November the 5th and 7th Marine regiments began their break-out through the CCF divisions encircling them. The Marines' goal was to link up with the divisional headquarters at Hagaru-ri which they reached on 4 December. When questioned by a war correspondent if the 1st Marine Division was retreating in the face of the enemy, its commander Major General Oliver P. Smith replied: 'Retreat hell, we're attacking in another direction.'

An example of what it took for the Marines to break out of the encircling CCF divisions between 30 November and 4 December appears in the following passage. It is from Lieutenant Colonel Raymond G. Davis's Medal of Honor citation, recognizing his actions between 1 and 4 December:

> Although keenly aware the operation involved breaking through a surrounding enemy and advancing 8 miles along primitive icy trails in the bitter cold with every passage disputed by a savage and determined foe, Lt. Col. Davis boldly led his battalion into the attack in a daring attempt to relieve a beleaguered rifle company and to seize, hold, and defend a vital mountain pass controlling the only route available for two Marine regiments in danger of being cut off by numerically superior hostile forces during their re-deployment to the port of Hungnam.

In the process of reaching Hagaru-ri, the two Marine regiments lost 154 killed, 55 missing in action, 921 wounded and non-battles losses (mostly due to frostbite); this came to 1,130 men. Included in the Marine withdrawal were remnants of a US Army 7th Infantry Division task force. Assigned to the eastern half of the Chosin Reservoir, it had been demolished by the CCF between the evening of 27 November and 1 December, losing 2,815 out of an original 3,200 soldiers.

Playing an essential part in the 1st Marine Division's successful withdrawal from the Chosin Reservoir was Marine aviation. An example of their contribution appears in an extract from a USMC historical publication:

> During daylight hours when Corsairs were on station, the Chinese could not mass their troops to mount such attacks because when they tried, they would be immediately subjected to devastating airstrikes with napalm, bombs, rockets, and overwhelming 20mm strafing. Not one enemy mass attack was delivered against the column during daylight hours.

At night, Marine aviation flew 'heckler' missions aimed at enemy artillery, mortar and heavy machine-gun firing positions located by the pilots flying over the Marine columns, observing their fire in the darkness of night.

Upon reaching Hagaru-ri, the Marines were able to fly out 4,316 casualties from an airfield that the 1st Marine divisional commander had insisted on being built. Flown in were 537 Marine replacements.

On 6 December the 5th and 7th Marine regiments began withdrawing from Hagaru-ri and heading towards the 1st Marine Regiment's perimeter, located 11 miles south at Koto-ri. It involved moving about 10,000 men and around 1,000 vehicles. On 8 December, the 1st Marine Division set forth on the last leg of its journey from Koto-ri, heading towards the port of Hungnam.

Not wanting to see the two Marine regiments escape, the CCF blew a 16ft gap in a critical section of road that they needed to pass over to complete their withdrawal. A US Army historical publication described how this dangerous situation was solved:

> The staff of X Corps coordinated an airdrop on 7 December of eight 2.25-ton Treadway bridge sections to cross the gap. In a series of air operations, all eight sections were dropped by parachute near the pass, with one falling inside Chinese lines and another damaged in the drop. However, the remaining sections bridged the gap and, despite some tense moments when trucks almost slid off the narrow bridge, the way was clear.

Arrival

In the afternoon of 11 December all the 1st Marine Division passed through defensive lines established by the US Army 3rd Infantry Division of X Corps around the port of Hungnam. In that phase of their withdrawal from 8 to 11 December, they reported 75 men dead, 16 missing in action and 256 wounded.

The CCF failure to pursue the 1st Marine Division during its withdrawal into Hungnam centred on several reasons. These included their high combat casualties, poor mobility due to insufficient motor transportation and Marine ground-support air power, as well as US Navy shipboard fire-power.

The commanding general of the 1st Marine Division had thought that his division would go into the defensive perimeter around the port city upon its arrival. However, the X Corps commander believed that the division's combat effectiveness was low and therefore ordered that it be the first out by ship. The US Army 7th Infantry Division was next, and last out the US Army 3rd Infantry Division. Also evacuated were X Corps' ROKA divisions and a large number of Korean civilians.

In the afternoon of 11 December, the 1st Marine Division sailed from Hungnam to Pusan, where it found itself reassigned from the X Corps to EUSA reserve, effective on 27 December. The latter was now under the command of US Army Lieutenant General Matthew B. Ridgway. He assumed command upon Lieutenant General Walker's death in a traffic accident on 23 December in South Korea.

MacArthur would eventually comment on a Marine Corps' study done on the fighting at the Chosin Reservoir:

> The Marine Corps Board of Study rightfully points out that the campaign of the 1st Marine Division with attached army elements in North Korea was 'largely

---

Evaluation of Major General Almond's X Corps Performance

In a US Army historical publication titled *Staff Operations: The X Corps in Korea, December 1950* by Dr Richard W. Stewart appears this conclusion on his study of Major General Almond's X Corps staff performance during a very critical period:

> The race to the Yalu and the Chosin Reservoir campaign were painful defeats because, to a great extent, X Corps did not follow its own doctrine of foreseeing events and planning for all contingencies. The corps jeopardized its operations and almost presented the EUSA and the US Government with a catastrophic defeat due to its lack of vision. The Far Eastern Command and General MacArthur must share in this blame, but the X Corps was the controlling headquarters and could have done more to analyze and plan for different contingencies.
>
> The recovery of the situation after the disastrous defeats of late November and early December were partly a result of X Corps remembering how a corps should act. The evacuation of Hungnam was a considerable triumph because X Corps recalled its proper role and coordinated as a corps should.

responsible for preventing reinforcement of CCF forces on Eighth Army front by 12 divisions during a period when such reinforcement might have meant to Eighth Army the difference between maintaining a foothold in Korea or forced evacuation from there.'

Others have suggested that having both the 1st Marine Division and the US Army 7th Infantry Division attached to the EUSA on the western side of the Peninsula would have prevented its collapse on 25 November and its subsequent rout.

MacArthur is shown here coming aboard the US Navy battleship *Missouri* (BB-63) a few days after the Inchon landings. With the success of Operation CHROMITE, MacArthur's standing was at its peak. For whatever reasons, MacArthur therefore decided that a major amphibious landing at the North Korean port of Wonsan would be as successful as it was at Inchon. (*US Navy*)

The port of Wonsan was located 80 miles north of the 38th Parallel and had the best deep-water harbour in all of Korea. Its appeal to MacArthur must have been its accessible harbour and nearby high-capacity airfield and its location that intersected major railroad and highways leading to the west and the North Korean capital of Pyongyang. (USMC)

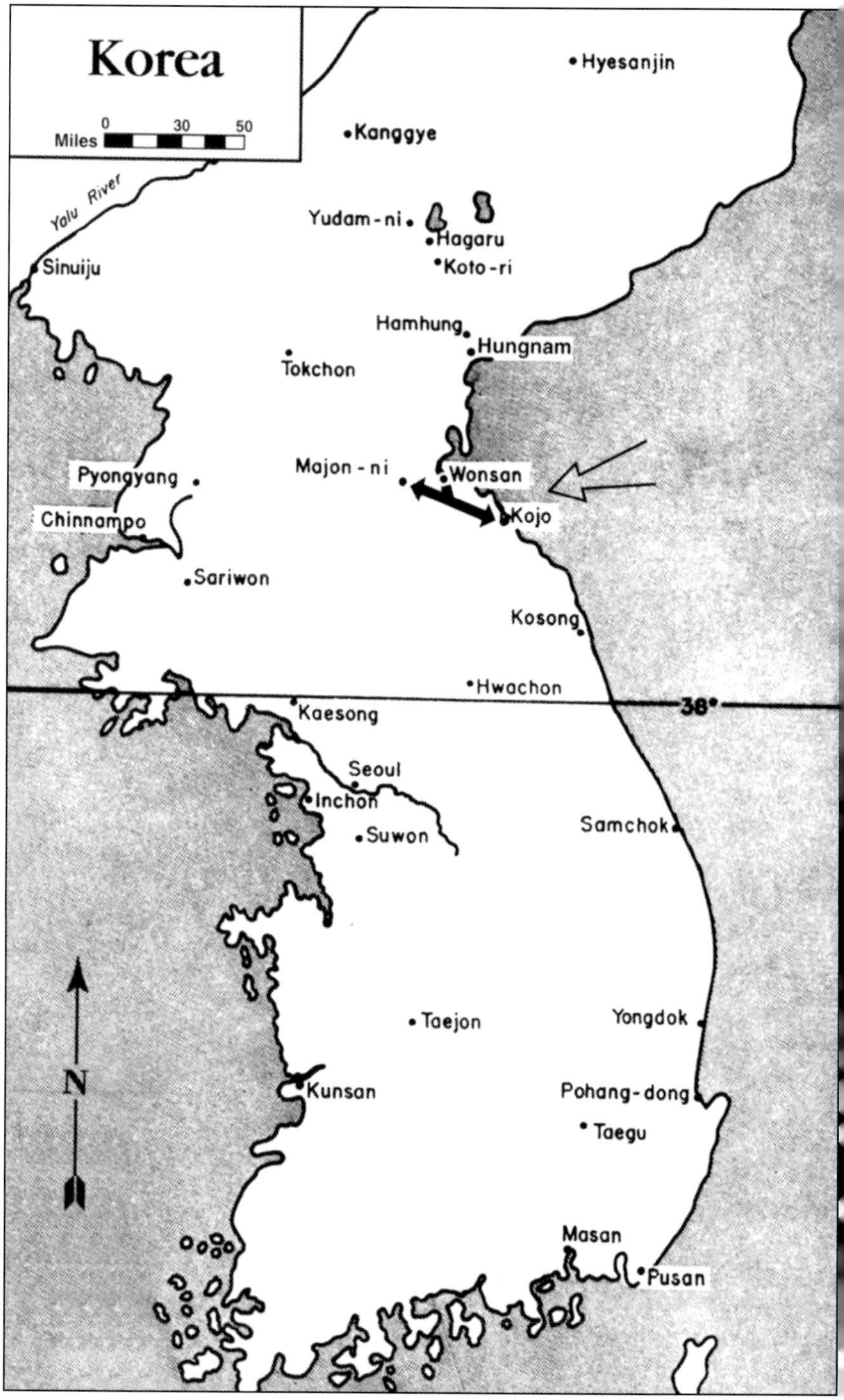

Korea

Miles 0 30 50

• Hyesanjin

• Kanggye

Yalu River

Yudam-ni •
• Hagaru

Sinuiju
• Koto-ri

Hamhung
• Hungnam

Tokchon

Pyongyang •
Majon-ni •
• Wonsan

Chinnampo
• Kojo

• Sariwon

Kosong

• Hwachon

Kaesong
38°

Seoul
• Inchon

Samchok

• Suwon

N

• Taejon
Yongdok

Kunsan
Pohang-dong
• Taegu

Masan
• Pusan

(**Opposite, above**) Reflecting its importance to the North Korean economy, Wonsan found itself subjected to aerial attacks before MacArthur's plans for the amphibious invasion of the port city came about. On 18 July 1950, US Navy carrier aircraft attacked a Wonsan oil facility. The attack reportedly destroyed some 12,000 tons of refined petroleum products, with the resulting smoke being visible 60 miles out to sea. (US Navy)

(**Opposite, below**) MacArthur did not unveil his plan to mount an amphibious assault on Wonsan to his subordinates until 29 September 1950. Upon being alerted to MacArthur's plans, the US Navy massed a number of its warships to commence a pre-invasion bombardment of the port. Here is an artist's rendition of a US Navy destroyer engaging enemy coastal artillery positions at Wonsan. (US Navy)

(**Above**) One can only suppose that MacArthur expected that an amphibious invasion of Wonsan would be as great a surprise to the North Korean military leadership as that at Inchon. That would not be the case, and with the assistance of Soviet military advisors, more than 2,000 mines were laid in the approaches to the port of Wonsan after the Inchon landings. Pictured here are US Navy minesweepers. (*US Navy*)

(**Opposite, above**) In this image, we see the moment at which a South Korean manned minesweeper set off an enemy mine. Several UN minesweepers were lost clearing the approaches to Wonsan. The US Navy senior leadership wondered why MacArthur even wanted to mount an amphibious invasion at Wonsan as the X Corps could drive across the Korean Peninsula in less time on a first-class highway. (*US Navy*)

(**Opposite, below**) To speed up the process of clearing the approaches to the port of Wonsan, the US Navy employed its Underwater Demolition Teams (UDTs), as seen here at a beach near the city. In addition to the UDTs, the US Navy tried to use its twin-engine, prop-driven Patrol Bomber, Martin #5 (PBM-5) Mariners to destroy mines with gunfire, a course of action that did not prove effective. (*US Navy*)

(**Above**) The commander of the US Navy attack force assigned to deliver the 1st Marine Division to Wonsan had come up with a novel idea to clear the enemy minefields. It involved aircraft dropping 1,000lb bombs and anti-submarine depth-charges (as pictured here) on the minefields themselves. The hope was that they would create enough overpressure to detonate nearby mines; however, it failed to accomplish the desired results. (*US Navy*)

(**Opposite, above**) The map illustrates the two landing beaches that would be used to bring the initial elements of the 1st Marine Division ashore on 26 October 1950, as well as the area cleared of mines to allow for their approaches to the selected beaches. The 1st Marine Division was assigned the capture of Wonsan on 4 October 1950, with the landing date initially set for 15 October 1950 but delayed due to the seaborne minefields. (*USMC*)

(**Opposite, below**) A picture taken inside a US Navy landing craft bringing Marines of the 1st Division to one of two landing sites near the port city of Wonsan. The landings were unopposed as the ROKA had secured the city on 10 October 1950; an occurrence predicted by many, making the entire amphibious operation unnecessary. Marine aircraft had flown into Wonsan airfield beginning on 13 October 1950. (*US Navy*)

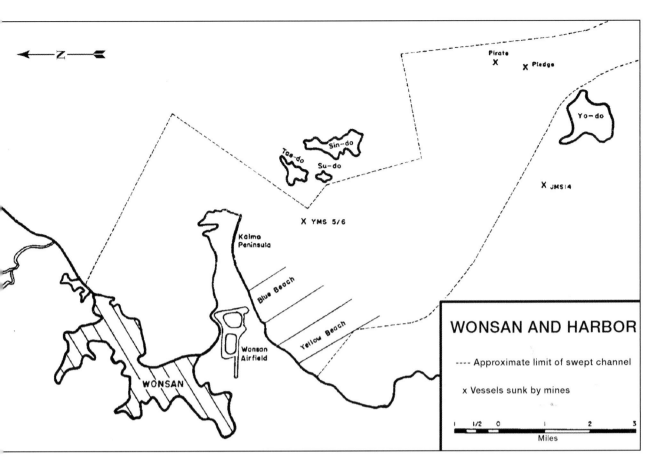

WONSAN AND HARBOR

---- Approximate limit of swept channel

x Vessels sunk by mines

Kalma
Peninsula

Blue Beach

Yellow Beach

Wonsan
Airfield

WONSAN

Tas-do   Sin-do
    Su-do

Yo-do

Pirate
X   X Pledge

X JMS14

X YMS 5/6

1st Division Marines shortly after their initial landing near the port city of Wonsan on 26 October 1950. Before the landings the Marines were stuck on their transport ships for three weeks, sailing back and forth along the coast of eastern Korea waiting for the enemy minefields to be cleared before they could disembark. The Marines on the ships sarcastically nicknamed their time at sea as 'Operation Yo-Yo'. (US Navy)

80-G-421376

Seen here during the Wonsan operation are Marine DUKWs (nicknamed 'Ducks') loaded with 105mm howitzers on board an LST (Landing Ship Tank). Reloading the 1st Marine Division at Inchon onto their transport ships intended for the Wonsan landing turned into a fiasco. What the X Corps' commander had anticipated would take only three days would actually take a week. (*USMC*)

Besides US Navy landing craft of various types and sizes, some of the 1st Division Marines were landed at Wonsan by LVT-3s. The example pictured here is in the original Second World War configuration. It had a cargo capacity of 9,000lb or could carry thirty standing passengers in its rear compartment. Top speed in the water was approximately 6 mph and about 17 mph on land. (*Patton Museum*)

125

As the Marines of the 1st Division moved inland after their beach landings near Wonsan, they were met by jeers and obscene jokes from Marine aviators and air crew as well as ROKA soldiers who arrived before they had. In this image we see 1st Marine Division infantrymen moving inland past the Wonsan airfield with an F4U-4 Corsair in the foreground. *(USMC)*

A Marine Corps M26 Pershing medium tank, still fitted with its wading gear, is parked near the Wonsan airfield, as is evident from the USAF C-54 transport plane seen in the background. The bulk of the tank-versus-tank engagements during the Korean War occurred between August and October 1950. From November 1950 onward there would be little or no combat between the opposing sides' armies. *(USMC)*

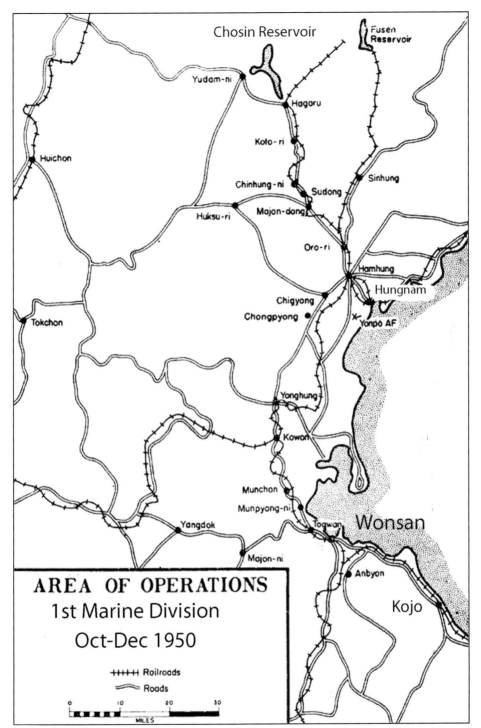

Chosin Reservoir

Fusen Reservoir

Yudam-ni

Hagaru

Koto-ri

Huichon

Chinhung-ni   Sinhung

Sudong

Huksu-ri   Majon-dong

Oro-ri

Tokchon   Chigyong

Chongpyong   Hamhung

Hungnam

Yonpo AF

Yonghung

Kowon

Munchon

Munpyong-ni

Yangdok   Togwon   Wonsan

Majon-ni   Anbyon   Kojo

AREA OF OPERATIONS
1st Marine Division
Oct-Dec 1950

++++++ Railroads
Roads

0   10   20   30
MILES

This map identifies various objectives assigned to the 1st Marine Division upon its arrival at Wonsan beginning on 26 October 1950. The division's main goal was to advance northward along the eastern coast of North Korea to the port of Hungnam with the 5th and 7th Marine regiments, and then to turn north-west and secure the Chosin Reservoir along with elements of the US Army 7th Infantry Division. (USMC)

The 1st Marine Regiment found itself assigned to rear-area security duties at Wonsan. One of the regiment's battalions went off to a ROKA supply depot located 40 miles south of the port at the North Korean coastal town of Kojo. Attacked by an undetected regiment of NKPA infantry on the night of 28 October 1950, it suffered heavy casualties in the process. A wounded Marine is shown here being carried to safety by stretcher-bearers. (USMC)

A Marine casualty is seen here going into an HO3S-1 observation helicopter. The HO3S-1's main role in the war became rapid aerial medical evacuation. A bench seat behind the helicopter's single pilot could accommodate three seated passengers or a single stretcher case, as seen in this picture. The type also saw use in rescuing downed pilots behind enemy lines. (*USMC*)

By the end of 1950, the HO3S-1 observation helicopter would be replaced in the aerial medical evacuation role in the Marine Corps by the HTL-4 helicopter pictured here. It could carry a stretcher patient on each of its two skids, doubling its payload. The helicopter had a cruising speed of 60 mph and a range of 150 miles. In US Army and USAF service it bore the designation H-13. (*USMC*)

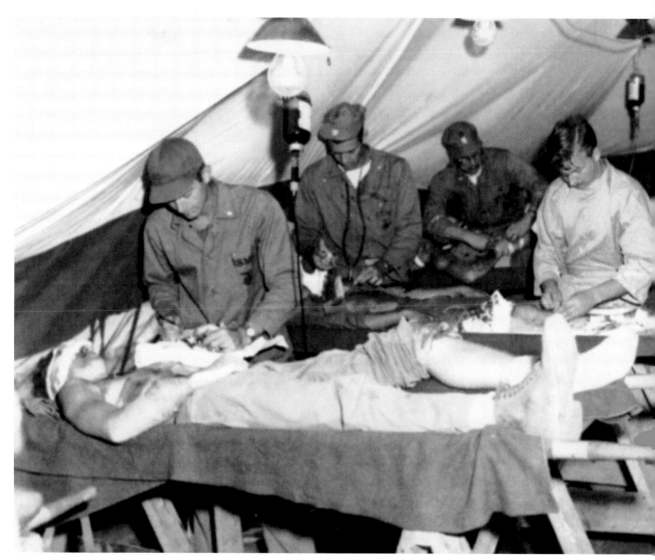

(**Above**) The Marine Corps has always depended on the US Navy for its medical personnel. At the lowest level, there were forty enlisted corpsmen assigned to each Marine infantry battalion. Depending on the seriousness of his wounds, a casualty might be sent back to a battalion aid station (BAS), typically consisting of a simple tent with the patients' stretchers placed upon pairs of sawhorses as pictured for initial treatment. (*US Navy*)

(**Opposite, above**) If the medical crew of a battalion aid station (BAS) could not deal with a Marine's wounds, the patient would go back to a temporary sixty-bed mobile field hospital labelled a 'Med' by the US Navy and a 'MASH' in US Army parlance. Pictured here is a US Army MASH facility. From there they might be transported to a semi-permanent division hospital. If still requiring care, they went to a theatre-level hospital in Japan. (*US Army*)

(**Opposite, below**) At some point in late 1950, the 1st Marine Tank Battalion began receiving the M26A1 Pershing medium tank, an example of which is pictured here. The M26A1 model of the Pershing had a single-baffle muzzle brake, rather than the two-baffle muzzle brake of the M26. Also the M26A1 had a bore evacuator behind its single-baffle muzzle brake. (*Pierre-Olivier Buan*)

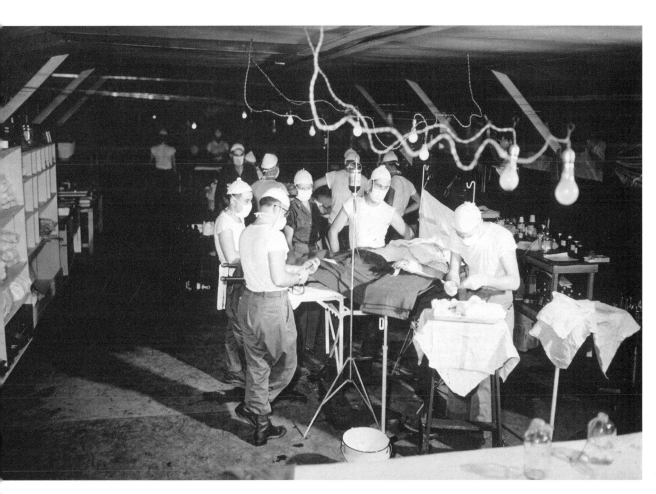

The Communist Chinese Army (CCF) began a major counteroffensive against the EUSA on the western side of the Korean Peninsula on 25 October 1950, leading to a collapse of the EUSA's front-line positions. On the western peninsula side of Korea, the ROKA divisions, belonging to X Corps, were the first to capture CCF soldiers, as pictured on 31 October 1951. (*USMC*)

Anticipating the upcoming Korean winter, the first issue of cold-weather gear for the 1st Marine Division took place at the end of October 1950. Pictured here are Marines from the 7th Regiment moving north to the port of Hungnam already seized by the ROKA. Only one of the Marines in the photograph is wearing a cold-weather parka with hood. (*USMC*)

About halfway to the Chosin Reservoir was the North Korean town of Sudong. On 2 November 1950, the 7th Marine Regiment replaced a ROKA regiment that had fought off a few small CCF patrols. What the Marines did not know at the time was that a CCF division of around 8,000 men surrounded them. Pictured here is a 105mm howitzer of the Marine 11th (Artillery) Regiment. (USMC)

On the night of 2 November 1950, the CCF division began a series of attacks on the 7th Marine Regiment. It took all the daylight hours of the 3rd before the Marines managed to eliminate the last of the CCF soldiers with the assistance of aircraft and artillery. The 11th Marine (Artillery) Regiment had one battalion armed with the 155mm howitzer seen here designated the M114. *(Pierre-Olivier Buan)*

The commander of the 1st Marine Air Wing 1st (MAW) that served alongside the 1st Marine Division during the Korean War was Major General Field Harris pictured here. He served in that role until the summer of 1951. In May 1945, he gave a speech on the topic of National Defense in which he stated: 'We are not an air force. We are a part of an air-ground team…. As always, we will aspire to be a useful and helpful arm of the United States Marines.' *(USMC)*

Marine pilots pose with a large bomb before another sortie against the enemy. Due to a lack of shipping, the majority of aircraft ground servicing equipment needed by the Marine squadrons flying out of the Wonsan airfield had been left behind in occupied Japan. Bombs, therefore, had to be attached to aircraft by muscle power and refuelled by small hand pumps. *(USMC)*

(**Above**) Pictured here is a dead CCF soldier; note the stick grenades in a belt bag. A Marine Corps historical publication describes the CCF, also referred to as the People's Liberation Army (PLA), as 'a massive, mostly illiterate, peasant army … its sheer size and vast combat experience made it a formidable foe.' All Chinese soldiers deployed to North Korea received the title 'volunteer', allowing Red China to deny its official involvement in the conflict. (*USMC*)

(**Opposite, above**) A small-arms weapon that equipped both the NKPA and CCF soldiers was the PPSh-1941 shown here. Designed and built in the Soviet Union during the Second World War for the Red Army, millions were produced. A simple blowback-operated weapon, it came with the seventy-one-round drum magazine pictured here or a thirty-five-round box magazine. Due to its high rate of fire, American soldiers and Marines referred to it as the 'Burp Gun'. (*US Army*)

(**Opposite, below**) A wounded Marine of the 7th Regiment awaits medical evacuation. Typically, he would have to be hand-carried down to the closest road and loaded on a truck that would transport him to an aid station. Helicopter evacuation remained rare. Total Marine losses on 2 and 3 November 1950 were 44 killed, 5 dead of wounds, 1 missing and 162 wounded. (*USMC*)

(**Opposite, above**) On 4 November 1950, the 7th Marine Regiment discovered that except for a few men, the CCF division that had attacked them from 2 to 4 November 1950 had withdrawn. The Marines were, however, surprised to encounter five NKPA T-34 medium tanks that day. In a wild melee, all five enemy tanks were dispatched with a combination of 75mm recoilless rifles (pictured), 3.5in rocket-launchers and aircraft. (*USMC*)

(**Opposite, below**) With the CCF division's withdrawal on 4 November 1950, the 7th Marine Regiment along with the 5th Marine Regiment continued to its objective, the Chosin Reservoir. On 5 November 1950, the Marines once again encountered the CCF with fighting continuing until the morning of 7 November 1950, when the CCF withdrew. Pictured here is a Marine M26A1 Pershing medium tank and supporting infantry. (*USMC*)

(**Above**) Marines are shown here checking a dwelling. On 5 November 1950, the Marines captured a stray CCF soldier who when interrogated told his captors that six CCF armies totalling twenty-four divisions had been committed to battle. When apprised of that news, the X Corps' commander expressed some concern. On 10 November 1950, the Korean winter began with a vengeance. One Marine stated that the cold seemed to 'numb the spirit as well as the flesh'. (*USMC*)

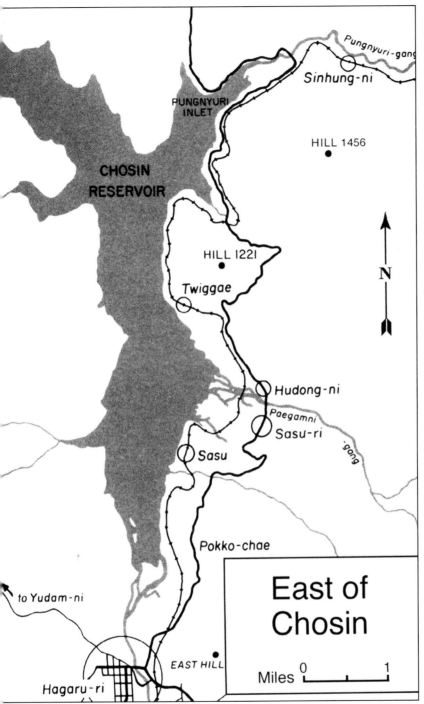

The 1st Marine Division reached the southern tip of the Chosin Reservoir on 16 November and by 25 November, had almost reached its northern tip. On 26 November the Marines captured several Red Chinese soldiers who stated that there were three CCF divisions nearby. In truth, there were twelve CCF divisions in the general area, amounting to 120,000 soldiers. (USMC)

(**Opposite, above**) With the cold came snow, making life for the Marines of the 1st Division near the Chosin Reservoir ever more miserable. In this photograph the Marines have constructed a warming tent with a makeshift stove and chimney. Some units claimed nighttime temperatures of 40 degrees below zero, with winds ranging from 35 to 40 mph. (USMC)

(**Opposite, below**) On the morning of 27 November 1950, the 1st Marine Division began advancing to the north-west from the Chosin Reservoir with the goal of relieving pressure on the EUSA which had been attacked by numerous CCF divisions on 25 November 1950. Whereas Marine artillery was all towed, the US Army had self-propelled artillery pieces, such as the M40 pictured here, armed with a 155mm howitzer. (US Army)

(**Opposite**) To the 1st Marine Division's senior leadership, the 27 November 1950 northward advance in the daylight hours made no sense at all as the EUSA on their left flank was already retreating, leaving the Marines' flank exposed. Their right flank was also unprotected. As the Marines moved forward, they quickly encountered CCF soldiers but with air support drove them off. Marines are shown here interrogating captured Chinese soldiers. (*USMC*)

(**Above**) The CCF soldiers encountered were equipped with an assortment of small arms from many different countries, including the American-designed and built M1A1 submachine gun seen here. The bulk of CCF soldiers encountered at the Chosin Reservoir were ex-Nationalist Chinese Army soldiers equipped by the United States before their surrender to the CCF in 1949. (*National Archives*)

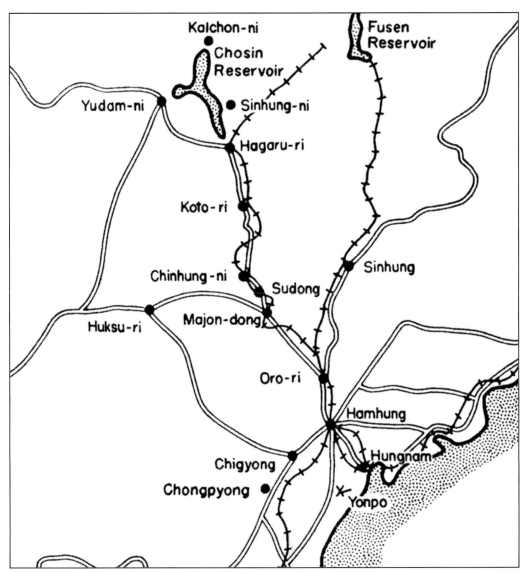

(**Above**) On the morning of 27 November 1950, the 1st Marine Division had all three of its infantry regiments in the same general area. The 5th and 7th Marine regiments were based at Yudam-ni on the western side of the Chosin Reservoir. Hagaru-ri was the 1st Marine Division headquarters and home to the 11th Marine (Artillery) Regiment, with Koto-ri the location of the 1st Marine Regiment. (*USMC*)

(**Opposite, above**) During the evening of 27 November 1950, the CCF launched a series of attacks on the 5th and 7th Marine regiments around Yudam-ni. Their attacks did not overrun the Marines' positions but did manage to cut the Marines' supply line to Hagaru-ri. The following day the enemy commander decided to halt his attack at Yudam-ni and concentrate on Hagaru-ri and Sinhung-ni. Marines are pictured here firing at encircling enemy soldiers. (*USMC*)

(**Opposite, below**) The Marines counterattacked to retake defensive positions lost to the CCF, without much success. On 29 November 1950, Marine tanks, pictured in conjunction with an assortment of truck-borne infantry, including British Marines and US Army soldiers, advanced out of Koto-ri in a failed attempt to push through to Hagaru-ri. (*USMC*)

(**Above**) On 28 November MacArthur ordered everyone to go on the defensive due to the CCF attacks on UN lines. The commander of the X Corps ordered all his divisions to withdraw to the port of Hungnam on 30 November. That same day the commanders of the two Marine regiments at Yudam-ni ordered a break-out to Hagaru-ri. Pictured here are Marines forming up a convoy in the brutal cold and winds of a Korean winter. (*USMC*)

(**Opposite, above**) A Marine scout/sniper aims at the enemy with his M1903A1 rifle fitted with an Unertl scope in this illustration. In fierce fighting the Marines of the 5th and 7th regiments broke out of the encircling CCF forces at Yudam-ni on 1 December and opened the road to Hagaru-ri. The last Marines departed Yudam-ni on 2 December. (*USMC*)

(**Opposite, below**) The first elements of the 5th and 7th Marine regiments reached Hagaru-ri on 3 December and the last on 4 December. During withdrawal, they had to endure constant enemy attacks and break through a succession of roadblocks. Pictured here are two Marine M4A3 medium tanks armed with 105mm howitzers. Visible on the lower front hulls of the tanks are the supporting fittings for bulldozer blades. (*USMC*)

(**Above**) Repeated CCF efforts to stop the Marine withdrawal from Yudam-ni to Hagaru-ri were beaten back with the help of Marine air support. Pictured here is a Marine forward air-control team guiding aircraft to their targets. Close air support requests of the most urgent nature were typically handled by aircraft on runway alert or by flights in the air on stand-by status. (USMC)

(**Opposite, above**) Be it at sea or the Wonsan airfield, cold-weather maintenance proved very difficult for those Marine squadrons supporting their comrades at the Chosin Reservoir. From a Marine historical publication is this passage: 'Aircraft engines had to be started throughout the night to keep them from freezing. Tyres on the planes would be frozen in the morning.' (USMC)

(**Opposite, below**) An artist's rendering of a rocket and napalm attack by Marine Corsairs during the fighting at the Chosin Reservoir. The CCF quickly discovered that they could not mount a large-scale daylight attack on the withdrawing Marine column without grievous losses from Marine aircraft. Even at night, Marine aircraft posed a threat to the CCF units, but not as serious as those in daylight. (USMC)

(**Opposite, above**) With the successful withdrawal of the 5th and 7th Marine regiments to the 1st Marine Division headquarters at Hagaru-ri on 4 December 1950, the on-site airfield was used to evacuate the wounded, both Marine and US Army. Due to the airfield's limited size, the largest transport plane that could land and take off was the twin-engine R4D-1 pictured here. In USAF service the aircraft was labelled the C-47. (*USMC*)

(**Opposite, below**) To aid in evacuation from the Koto-ri airfield of the wounded and those suffering from frostbite, the 1st MAG borrowed three of the US Navy's Second World War Avenger torpedo bombers as pictured here. Within the aircraft's large fuselage, it could carry three litter patients or as many as nine ambulatory cases. (*USMC*)

(**Above**) On 6 December the 5th and 7th Marine regiments began a break-out from Hagaru-ri to reach Koto-ri, the location of the 1st Marine Regiment. Pictured here are Marine M26A1 Pershing medium tanks. In spite of tough enemy resistance, the last elements of the two Marine regiments reached Koto-ri on the night of 7 December. (*USMC*)

(**Opposite, above**) A wartime artist's drawing of a Marine and his Browning Automatic Rifle (BAR) during the Korean War. From a US Army Korean War report is this passage on the weapon's usefulness: '… the BAR greatly compounds the stopping effect of rifle fire at ranges considerably in excess of those at which unaided rifle fire is potent. It has long been prized as a mop-up agent, for depressing final resistance in a conquered area, or liquidating tenacious elements infesting the rear.' (*USMC*)

(**Opposite, below**) The M114 155mm howitzers of the Marine 11th (Artillery) Regiment were towed by commercial tractors, as seen here during the withdrawal from the Chosin Reservoir. The CCF greatly feared American artillery as it accounted for more CCF casualties than any other ground weapon. The 1st Marine Division set forth on the last leg of its journey from Koto-ri, heading towards the port of Hungnam on 8 December. (*USMC*)

(**Above**) Due to heavy losses and their lack of mobility, the CCF could not keep up with the 1st Marine Division as it withdrew to the port of Hungnam. To slow the Marines down so that the CCF divisions could catch up with them, a concrete bridge at the Funchilin Pass was blown by the enemy, as pictured here, as well as two improvised replacement bridges. The solution: the USAF air-dropped a replacement bridge that went into use on 9 December. (*USMC*)

(**Above**) A Marine infantryman shows off a poster of Soviet dictator Joseph Stalin he found within an abandoned CCF bunker near the Funchilin Pass. The poster was no doubt brought to Korea by a Chinese Army political officer to inspire the men in his unit. With the collapse of the CCF logistical system during the Battle for the Chosin Reservoir, the typical Chinese soldier was no doubt more interested in food and warm clothing. (*USMC*)

(**Opposite, above**) A wartime artist's drawing of Marines escorting a wounded comrade to an aid station. US Navy corpsmen in the field often kept morphine packets in their mouths during fire-fights to keep them warm enough for injection. Company-level corpsmen erected warming tents whenever possible to temporarily house exhausted and lightly-wounded Marines. (*USMC*)

(**Opposite, below**) During the Battle of the Chosin Reservoir, starting in late November 1950 and continuing into mid-December 1950, the Marine Corps HO3S-1 helicopters continued to prove their worth, despite unforgiving flying conditions. Besides enemy anti-aircraft fire, there was the problem of flying helicopters at very high altitudes in thin air and brutal weather conditions. (*USMC*)

(**Above**) The Marines who died while fighting in the many hills that marked the Chosin Reservoir were normally carried down on stretchers to the main roads. At that point, they went onto trucks that delivered them to the grave registration detachment of their particular regiment. The Marine dead pictured here are at Yudam-ni. *(USMC)*

(**Opposite, above**) During the last few days of the 1st Marine Division's withdrawal from the Chosin Reservoir to Hungnam, there appeared in support the first Marine fighter squadron equipped with jets, the F9F-2 Panther pictured here. The aircraft's maximum speed was 579 mph and its cruising speed 481 mph. Despite its speed advantage over the prop-driven Corsair, the Panther had a poor service reliability record. *(US Navy)*

(**Opposite, below**) On 8 December, the 1st Marine Division passed through the defensive perimeter established by the recently-arrived US Army 3rd Infantry Division around the port of Hungnam. Its men and equipment, as seen here, went onto ships between 9 and 10 December, with the division sailing to the port of Pusan on 11 December and arriving the same day. *(USMC)*

(**Opposite, below**) A Marine on a ship departing the port of Hungnam and going to Pusan guards two very bewildered-looking Chinese soldiers. A Marine Corps historical publication describes the typical CCF soldier as being 'thoroughly indoctrinated, but once taken prisoner that indoctrination would tend to crack', and went on to say they were 'surprisingly docile and uncomplaining once captured'. *(USMC)*

Upon the last elements of the X Corps departing the port of Hungnam on 24 December, it was destroyed by the American military as shown here to deny its use by the NKPA or the CCF. During the seaborne evacuation from Hungnam, aerial coverage came from seven US Navy aircraft carriers. Naval gunfire support came from US Navy warships ranging from battleships to destroyers. (*US Navy*)

Chapter Four

Back and Forth

O n the ships evacuating the 1st Marine Division from the North Korean port of Hungnam on 15 and 16 December, some thought they might be returning to Japan or the United States. That idea did not last long as most disembarked from their transport ships at Pusan the same day. Those that did not were transported by smaller vessels to the South Korean port city of Masan. The Marines landed at Pusan were moved to Masan by trucks and trains.

The commander of the EUSA envisioned employing the Marines in his reserve force for two roles: first to hold open a corridor to Pusan, and second to act as a rearguard if the latest enemy offensive, launched on 31 December and referred to by historians as the CCF 'third phase offensive', succeeded and forced the UN to evacuate from Pusan. Fortunately, the enemy offensive was brought to a halt in mid-January 1951 by the EUSA.

Cleaning Up

During the fighting that took place during the CCF third phase offensive, an NKPA division passed through an opening in the ROKA lines. That opening was quickly plugged, leaving the enemy division cut off along the east coast of the Korean Peninsula in a location referred to as the 'Pohang area'. To maximize their impact, the enemy commander divided his division into smaller units and turned to guerrilla warfare.

Because the enemy's presence posed a danger to an important UN supply line and airfield, the 1st Marine Division (still in the EUSA reserve force) received orders to move to the location on 8 January, encountering elements of the NKPA division on 18 January. In that engagement and subsequent fighting, the enemy suffered heavy casualties. By 11 February the 1st Marine Division commander reported to the EUSA commander '… the situation in the division area is sufficiently in hand to permit the withdrawal of the division and the assignment of another mission.'

A New Mission

In late January 1951, the 1st Marine Division commander met with the EUSA commander to talk about new missions. The former wanted to keep the 1st Marine

Division along the east coast of the Korean Peninsula for several reasons. These included the fact that it was the only UN division trained in amphibious operations; therefore it might prove valuable to keep that option open. The EUSA commander agreed and told his staff to make the necessary arrangements.

A new enemy offensive began on 11 February, labelled by historians as the CCF 'fourth phase offensive'. It soon made the arrangement of keeping the 1st Marine Division at its existing location moot and it found itself rushed to south-central Korea in response. At that point, it was transferred from EUSA reserve to IX Corps command. However, by the time the 1st Marine Division arrived in south-central Korea, the CCF fourth phase offensive had already been successfully blunted by the EUSA on 17 February.

The EUSA commanding general then incorporated the 1st Marine Division into a counterattack labelled Operation KILLER launched on 20 February. Its objective was the destruction of CCF and NKPA forces located north and east of Seoul. With that task completed, the EUSA could then begin advancing to the 38th Parallel. Unfortunately, the bulk of the enemy forces withdrew successfully in the face of the EUSA's advance.

Operation KILLER was followed by Operation RIPPER that began on 7 March. Its goal, like that of Operation KILLER, was to inflict maximum casualties on the enemy and maintain constant pressure on his front-line positions. A secondary goal would be the securing of 'real estate' and by doing so, outflanking the enemy-occupied city of Seoul and cutting the enemy's supply lines in the area. The EUSA took Seoul on 14 March. By the time Operation RIPPER concluded, the Marines had suffered 558 casualties and accounted for about 3,000 enemy casualties.

On a Roll

With the partial success of Operations KILLER and RIPPER, the EUSA commander wanted to push his divisions across the 38th Parallel and at least 20 miles into North Korea before establishing new defensive lines. The result was two more operations labelled RUGGED and DAUNTLESS. The former lasted from 2 to 11 April. The latter began on 9 April with the goal achieved on 22 April.

Rather than enemy units slowing down the Marine 1st Division as well as other EUSA divisions, it was rough terrain, craters and debris from friendly artillery and air strikes blocking roads. Another threat came from land mines, especially anti-tank (AT) mines, as seen in this passage from a US Army report dated 1951:

> Minefields encountered were of irregular pattern and of various sizes. As a rule, AT mines were laid in pairs, one mine on each side of the road. These mines were laid the same width as our tank tracks thereby engaging both tank tracks simultaneously. In some instances, three (3) or four (4) mines would be placed

upon each other in order to give them more power. Many vehicles were lost by hitting mines that were laid on the shoulders of the roads.

Despite the EUSA's success in pushing about 20 miles into North Korea during Operations RUGGED and DAUNTLESS, its commander reminded his corps commanders to be wary of an enemy counteroffensive and be ready to fall back to prepared defensive lines north of Seoul.

We're Back

On 22 April, the CCF launched another offensive. Historians label it as the 'first step' of the CCF's 'fifth phase offensive'. As almost always, they aimed their attacks on the weakest units in the EUSA's defensive lines, ROKA divisions, one of which had been assigned to guard the left flank of the 1st Marine Division.

A US Army report dated May 1952 had this to say about the ROKA: 'South Korean troops demonstrated themselves as unreliable in combat. A unit that fought bravely against overwhelming odds in one engagement would disintegrate before an inferior force in another.'

With the collapse of the ROKA division on the Marines' left flank, the CCF divisions went on to punch a 10-mile penetration into the EUSA zone of responsibility, leaving the 1st Marine Division outflanked and its supply lines threatened.

At about 2.00 am on 23 April in the morning darkness, the CCF finally reached the Marines' lines. This assault's opening is described as follows in a USMC historical publication: 'Shrieking whistles, clanging cymbals, and blasting bugles signaled the onslaught. Up and down the line grizzled veterans of the Chosin Reservoir walked the lines to settle down young Marines who had not yet experienced a terrifying "human wave" ground assault.'

Marine supporting arms aided in breaking up the CCF's initial attack as well as subsequent attempts to overrun the Marines' defensive positions. With the morning light of 23 April, the CCF units hurriedly departed from the area as they knew that

Enemy Attacks

During the Korean War the American press, as well as USMC reports, often described Red Chinese Army attacks as consisting of human-wave assaults. A favourite term used was 'horde'. The favourite joke among American troops during the Korean War was 'How many hordes are there in a Chinese platoon?'

From a Korean War US Army report by historian S.L.A. Marshall is this description of the typical CCF ground-attack formation employed against UN troops:

> The Chinese do not characteristically employ mass, for example, in the way that the Red Army used it against the Germans in operations in the Ukraine during World War II, coming on in such numbers that the human sea absorbed and ultimately smothered the fire volume. Rather, in the attack, CCF tend to move against our works in multiple, thin lines, well-spaced each from the other, after having deployed out of column in the last phase of the approach. The approach column may be single file, or even a regiment moving four abreast, depending on the situation and the size of the attack force.

Marine aviation would soon be on the scene. They moved a bit too slowly that morning, and the gull-winged Corsairs swooped upon their prey and accounted for a high number of enemy dead.

In spite of their losses to the 1st Marine Division, the CCF units continued to pour through the front-line positions abandoned by the ROKA division on the 1st Marines' left flank. A Marine officer commented that the setting was 'very similar to the situation at the Chosin Reservoir'. Despite the CCF repeatedly trying to outflank the 1st Marine Division on the nights of 24 and 25 April, they were unsuccessful.

Backing Up

In the face of continued CCF attacks along the EUSA's entire front-line positions, the commanding officer ordered that all his divisions, including the 1st Marine Division, withdraw rearward to a newly-built defensive line referred to as the 'No Name Line'. The retrograde movement began on 26 April and was completed by 30 April in good order with no breakdowns in discipline and unit cohesion.

The only enemy soldier encountered by the Marines during their pull-back appears in a USMC historical publication: '... one bewildered Chinese straggler who had inadvertently fallen in with the Marine column in the darkness. He was more than somewhat surprised to discover himself among several thousand Americans when daylight came.'

Unlike the enemy offensives that had occurred in 1950 that had routed the EUSA on two different occasions, the enemy offensive that began in April 1951 failed to induce the panic sarcastically referred to by American personnel as 'bug-out fever'.

The enemy offensive eventually collapsed on the No Name Line. They had, however, recovered all the ground the EUSA had gained during Operations RUGGED and DAUNTLESS.

Transferred Once Again

At the start of May 1951, the enemy seemed to be directing its attention to X Corps' defensive lines on the eastern side of the Korean Peninsula. In response, the EUSA transferred the 1st Marine Division from IX Corps back to X Corps. On 12 May, US Army General Mark Clark replaced General Ridgway as theatre commander.

On the night of 16 May, the CCF launched an assault on X Corps referred to by historians as the 'second step of their fifth phase offensive'. Once again the CCF directed its attacks against a ROKA division that quickly gave way. The enemy soon created a 20-mile-deep penetration in the corps' lines. The 1st Marine Division counterattacked and by 20 May the enemy had been repulsed. By 30 May, the EUSA and X Corps had recaptured much of the terrain lost to the enemy counteroffensive.

The X Corps' commanding officer congratulated the Marines for their accomplishment '... of a most arduous battle task. You have denied [the enemy] the

---

Problems with the Fifth Air Force

The 1st Marine Division's unhappiness with the Fifth Air Force taking control of the land-based elements of the 1st MAW in October 1950 had become part of an inter-service controversy by the spring of 1951. On one side was the Marine Corps (as well as the X Corps commander), and on the other side, the United States Air Force (USAF).

The major sticking-point between the two sides was that the USAF had no interest in providing close air support. USAF senior leadership regarded it as both dangerous and wasteful of its aerial assets. The USAF saw air superiority and interdiction as its primary roles. Unfortunately for the Marine Corps, both General Ridgway, the theatre commander, and the EUSA commander concurred with the USAF.

The USAF believed that artillery fulfilled the close-support role required by the US Army and Marine ground forces in combat. The US Marine Corps, on the other hand, had long regarded the close air support mission as essential for its ground combat operations, complementing artillery support.

The X Corps commander and the 1st Marine Division commander complained heartily about the arrangement to their superiors, as well as to the USAF. In response, a single squadron was reassigned to X Corps, and its missions still required Fifth Air Force's approval. The running joke among the Marines was that they had to fight three enemies: the North Koreans, the Chinese and the USAF.

opportunity of regrouping his forces and forced him into a hasty retreat; the destruction of enemy forces and material has been tremendous and many times greater than our own losses.'

Forward Once Again

The day after the enemy assault (the second step of their fifth phase offensive) came to an end, the EUSA commander ordered a counterattack on a broad front across the entire Korean Peninsula. The 1st Marine Division's assigned objective was to secure a portion of an area referred to as 'the Punchbowl'. It was an ancient volcanic crater ringed by steep hills and defended by the NKPA, which at that time proved a tougher opponent than the CCF.

The Marines' advance began on 1 June, attacking the Punchbowl on 2 June. From a USMC historical publication: 'All day long, Marine squads inched upwards through the [enemy] bunker complex, eventually destroying the bunkers with grenades and satchel charges. In one case a lone Marine jumped into a bunker, killed three North Koreans with his rifle and strangled the fourth with his bare hands.'

The fighting for the Punchbowl continued into the third week of June, with the 1st Marine Division badly bloodied but having secured its goal. Marine losses were 183 dead and 1,973 wounded, which exceeded those at the Chosin Reservoir. A Marine officer present recalled 'it was the toughest fighting I have ever seen.'

A Pause in the Fighting

By the end of June 1951, X Corps' commanding officer informed the 1st Marine Division's commander that his men would no longer conduct major offensive operations. Instead, they would only be called upon to patrol in front of their existing defensive lines. By this time, 50 per cent of all the Marines in Korea were reservists.

This change in posture reflected talks among the combatants regarding a possible cease-fire. President Truman declared on 25 June: 'We are ready to join in a peaceful settlement in Korea now, as we have always been.' On orders from his civilian superiors, General Ridgway, the new theatre commander, broadcast over the radio on 30 June that the UN was willing to discuss an armistice.

In a USMC historical publication appears the following passage on what the enemy gained from temporary peace talks:

> The Soviets saw truce negotiations as a way to increase their influence in the United Nations as well as to buy time to rebuild and rearm the Chinese forces. The North Koreans – represented by the pestiferous Kim Il Sung – wanted only more war and no talks, unless a truce brought an end to American airstrikes.

In mid-July, the US Army 2nd Infantry Division took over the 1st Marine Division's front-line positions. The latter then became part of X Corps' reserve. Once in reserve, the Marine 1st Division commander began a robust training programme for his men. At the same time, he had all the division's equipment from radios to tanks rebuilt, with the help of US Army technicians.

New Plans

The EUSA's commander had, in anticipation of heavy fighting resuming at some point, broached the idea to the theatre commander of the 1st Marine Division of out-flanking the enemy's position with an amphibious operation behind their lines. This was to take place along the east coast of the Korean Peninsula and was referred to as Operation OVERWHELMING. Unfortunately, the theatre commander proved uninterested in his deputy's ideas.

US Army Major General Clovis E. Byers replaced Lieutenant General Almond as commander of X Corps in July 1951. He became very concerned in August of that year by growing signs of a significant enemy counteroffensive as the latest series of peace talks had ended that same month. These signs included a reduced number of civilian refugees, a reduction in enemy vehicle sightings and the enemy's imposition of radio silence. Also, the US Army 2nd Infantry Division and the ROKA divisions in X Corps' front lines were not making any progress in overcoming enemy defences.

Back into the Fray

Meetings between the new X Corps' commander and the EUSA's commander during 25 to 26 August resulted in a call to the 1st Marine Division commander. He was to use his division to replace a ROKA division at the Punchbowl. On 31 August, the EUSA ordered the entire X Corps to go over to the offensive. All the partici-pating divisions, including the 1st Marine Division, made slow going as the enemy's defensive works were extensive.

From a US Army report is a passage describing the enemy defensive system that the Marines of the 1st Division encountered at the Punchbowl:

> In sighting field fortifications, the enemy takes advantage of key hills which are suitable for all-around defense. Where possible the positions are constructed in-depth and are mutually supporting; alternate positions, terrain, and camouflage are all taken into account. The fields of fire covering slopes and draws show good coordination.

An indication of the intensity of the fighting appears in an extract from the Medal of Honor citation of Sergeant Frederick W. Mausert III. After a painful head wound on 10 September:

> [he] took the point position and led his men in a furious bayonet charge against the first of a literally impregnable series of bunkers. Stunned and knocked to the

ground when another bullet struck his helmet, he regained his feet and resumed his drive, personally silencing the machine-gun and leading his men in eliminating several other emplacements in the area.

Struck for a third time, he refused aid and continued leading his men forward and from his citation: 'Leaping into the wall of fire, he destroyed another machine-gun with grenades before he was mortally wounded by bursting grenades and machine-gun fire.'

Heavy losses suffered by the US Army 2nd Infantry Division (of the X Corps) in the Punchbowl area, nicknamed by civilian correspondents as 'Heartbreak Ridge', would lead the EUSA commander to end the 1st Marine Division's advance on 20 September. By doing so, he could direct all the X Corps' fire-support assets to aid the 2nd Infantry Division in its struggle to secure the ridge. That goal finally came about on 13 October 1951.

Going on the Defensive

On 7 October the opposing sides agreed to move a new round of armistice talks from Kaesong in southern North Korea to Panmunjom, located in North Korea closer to the 38th Parallel. Talks began at the latter site on 25 October. The American government was seeking an end to the fighting, as the growing list of casualties caused the American public to pull support from the war effort. The American military also preferred to devote its resources to the defence of Western Europe.

A Helicopter First

The 1st Marine Division and the 1st MAW took advantage of the lull in fighting during October 1951 by testing out its growing helicopter inventory in a new role. Rather than merely delivering wounded Marines to rear-area medical stations, helicopters would support the first large-scale movement of troops and their supplies from one location to another on 11 October in what became known as Operation BUMBLEBEE.

From a USMC historical publication is this description of the operation:

Twelve helicopters (HRS-1s) were employed in 156 flights to transport the 7th Marines from reserve to a landing site … just behind the 5th Marines MLR, north-east of Hill 702. A flight path of 15 miles took advantage of the concealment afforded by valleys and defiladed areas.

Ten to twelve minutes were required per flight … total weight of 229,920 pounds included 985 combat-equipped troops, averaging 240 pounds … Only four days later, HMR-161 demonstrated its ability to carry out on short notice an emergency resupply and evacuation operation in a combat zone.

The EUSA commander on 14 November issued orders to end all offensive operations at battalion level and above without permission from his headquarters. On 27 November orders came down halting any offensive operations for a month. As of 27 December, the EUSA halt order would go on indefinitely.

According to a USMC historical publication regarding the order of 27 December: '... it brought about few changes in the warfare of position which had replaced warfare of movement on 20 September. Each Marine Regiment on the MLR [main line of resistance] continued to send out several squad-size patrols nightly for such purposes as ambush, reconnaissance, and taking prisoners.'

For the last few days of 1951 and into early 1952, the Marines did their best to survive the bitter cold of another Korean winter. The 1st Marine Division, still under the command of X Corps, had the responsibility for a defensive area 14 miles across and 30 miles deep. Both the Marines and the enemy, despite the armistice talks, engaged in a constant non-stop series of small-scale battles, which included artillery barrages by both sides.

A Transfer Westward

On 12 March 1952, the EUSA commander decided that the 1st Marine Division would take the place of a ROKA division on the far western side of the Korean Peninsula. The Marine division would, in turn, be replaced by a ROKA division in the X Corps' defensive lines. The process was given the name Operation MIXMASTER.

In its move from the eastern side of the Korean Peninsula to its western side, completed on 25 March, the 1st Marine Division would pass from the control of X Corps to I Corps. The reason given for the relocation appears in a passage from a USMC historical publication:

(1) The abandonment of plans to carry out an amphibious envelopment somewhere on the east coast [of North Korea].

(2) Concern over weaknesses in the Kimpo area defenses [the historic invasion route to Seoul].

(3) The overall situation would not permit loss of ground on the EUSAK [EUSA] left (South Korea) as this would endanger the capital at Seoul; that if retraction of lines was necessary, territory could better be sacrificed on the right (North Korea) where the country was mountainous and had little economic or strategic value.

Upon its arrival, the 1st Marine Division took over a defensive line 30 miles long referred to as the 'Jamestown Line'. Instead of facing the NKPA, they now confronted the best divisions in the CCF totalling approximately 50,000 men. The Marines had about 30,000 men that included 4,400 South Korean Marines.

A new mission went to the 1st Marine Division on 19 April. It involved rescue of the UN truce negotiators if the enemy should try to trap them at Panmunjom, located about 5 miles from the 1st Marine Division's front lines.

The Fighting Kicks Up

With the coming of spring in early 1952, the CCF became ever more aggressive, with the Marines of the 1st Division responding in kind. An example of the fighting and dying along the Jamestown Line appears in the Medal of Honor citation of Marine Corporal Duane E. Dewey:

> ... in action against enemy aggressor forces near Panmunjom, Korea, on April 16, 1952. When an enemy grenade landed close to his position while he and his assistant gunner were receiving medical attention for their wounds during a fierce night attack by numerically superior hostile forces, Corporal Dewey, although suffering intense pain, immediately pulled the corpsman to the ground and, shouting a warning to the other Marines around him, bravely smothered the deadly missile with his body, personally absorbing the full force of the explosion to save his comrades from possible injury or death.

In July 1952, I Corps' commander ordered the 1st Marine Division to conduct a series of large-scale raids to gather more information about enemy defensive positions. The

---

Changes in US Army Leadership

On 11 April 1951, President Truman relieved General MacArthur from his command. There were several reasons for this action. These included the latter's desire to widen the Korean War by bombing the Soviet Union and Red China as well as involving Nationalist Chinese Forces in the conflict. Truman would later write that 'General MacArthur was willing to risk general war [Third World War]; I was not.'

General of the US Army Omar N. Bradley and chairman of the JCS stated that if MacArthur had been given his way in the Korean conflict, it would have resulted in 'the wrong war, at the wrong time, at the wrong place, and with the wrong enemy.' The Soviet Union was considered the main enemy at that time.

Lieutenant General Ridgway took over MacArthur's command positions on 14 April 1951, and at the same time was promoted to general. US Army Lieutenant General James A. Van Fleet assumed command of the EUSA, which included the 1st Marine Division.

On 12 May 1952, General Mark W. Clark replaced General Ridgway in MacArthur's former position. Ridgway had been named to replace General Dwight D. Eisenhower as the Supreme Commander, Allied Powers Europe, and head of the North Atlantic Treaty Organization (NATO), formed on 4 April 1949.

The Patton Tank

The newest Marine tank in Korea was the M46 Patton medium tank. Not a brand-new tank, it was a modernized version of the earlier M26 Pershing medium tank. It retained the 90mm main gun armed turret of its predecessor, but its hull featured a new more powerful engine and cross-drive transmission, providing it with an improved degree of off-road mobility.

On the less positive side there was a serious shortage of spare parts for the M46 Patton tank throughout its time in Korea. In addition, there was a lack of qualified personnel to operate them, so much so that the commanding officer of the 1st Marine Division had written to one of his superiors about the issue in July 1952:

> The other major shortage in the division was that of qualified crewmen — both drivers and gunners — for the M46 tanks. Neither tank driving nor gunnery for the M46 was taught in the tank crewmen's course conducted at Camp Pendleton, California … that tank crewmen should be thoroughly trained prior to leaving the US.

Some US Army reports at the time also mentioned the unavailability of spare parts for the M46 tanks as well as the absence of trained service personnel to keep them working.

commander of the 1st Marine Division believed that his MLR would be jeopardized by taking away his men for the proposed raids. He also believed that smaller patrols could achieve the same results with fewer casualties. Overruled, the first large raid against the CCF on 6 July involved a Marine tank-infantry team.

These large raids would continue through the remainder of 1952, with varying degrees of success. The first genuinely successful example occurred on 13 and 14 August when a Marine tank-infantry team undertook a nighttime attack on a CCF defensive position referred to by the Marines as 'Bunker Hill'.

From a USMC historical publication appears the following extract:

> One measure of the results of the Bunker Hill fighting is seen in the price paid. Chinese losses were estimated by the 1st Marine Division at approximately 3,200, including more than 400 known dead … The battle of Bunker Hill resulted in the first major Marine action and victory in West Korea. It ushered in two straight months of hard fighting, the most difficult ones yet for Marines on the western front.

One of the ships employed to evacuate the 1st Marine Division from the North Korean port of Hungnam is shown here arriving at the South Korean port of Pusan. It took four US Navy transport ships, sixteen US Navy Landing Ship Tanks (LSTs), a US Navy assault cargo ship and seven commercial merchant ships to move the 22,215 men of the division and their equipment to South Korea. *(US Navy)*

South Korean guards, trained by the US Navy, stand watch over the port of Pusan. Once the bulk of the 1st Marine Division arrived at Pusan on 16 December, it was transported by rail and truck to a large tent camp at the small South Korean port of Masan. Of the division's 4,418 casualties suffered between 26 October and 15 December, around half occurred in its three infantry regiments. *(US Navy)*

After four months of combat, the 1st Marine Division's stay at the Masan tent camp was a time for the men to recuperate and conduct refresher training, as seen in this photograph. Replacements, both men and equipment, also arrived during the division's stay. On 28 December the division was returned to the X Corps. *(USMC)*

Even as the 1st Marine Division arrived at Masan the war continued, with the EUSA retreating under strong CCF pressure. By the closing days of 1950 it appeared to some that the enemy might be on the verge of victory. In this picture we see a US Army-made sign indicating the 38th Parallel, which divided North and South Korea. (*US Army*)

A US Army soldier is shown here trying to stay warm. Such was the threat posed by the CCF divisions all along the EUSA defensive lines in early January 1951 that the 1st Marine Division was called back into action. Its job was to protect the EUSA's communication and supply line as well as stiffen the fighting resolve of some shaky ROKA divisions under intense CCF pressure. (*US Army*)

In late December 1950, US Army General Matthew B. Ridgway, pictured here, assumed command of the EUSA, which now included the 1st Marine Division. He replaced Lieutenant General Walton H. Walker, who was killed in a traffic accident on 23 December 1950. Ridgway is seen riding in the back of MacArthur's Jeep during a rare visit to Korea by the latter. (*US Army*)

US Army soldiers in Korea are using an M4A3(76)W tank as cover while engaging the enemy. Despite misgivings about General Ridgway, he managed in a few weeks to improve the fighting spirit of the EUSA. General of the US Army Omar N. Bradley, Chairman of the JCS, stated 'a battlefield turnaround unlike and within American history.' The corps had a small number of M4A3(76)W tanks, but did not use them during the Korean War. (*US Army*)

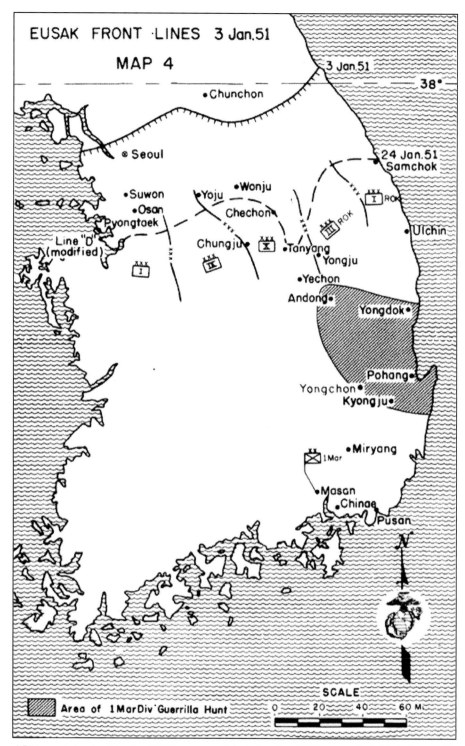

EUSAK FRONT LINES 3 Jan. 51

MAP 4

3 Jan. 51

38°

•Chunchon

⊗ Seoul

24 Jan. 51
Samchok

•Suwon

•Yoju

•Wonju

I ROK

•Osan

Chechon•

III ROK

Pyongtaek

Line "D"
(modified)

Chungju•

X

•Tanyang

•Ulchin

IX

•Yongju

I

•Yechon

Andong•

Yongdok•

Pohang•

Yongchon•

Kyongju•

1 Mar

•Miryang

•Masan

•Chinae

Pusan

N

SCALE

0   20   40   60 M.

Area of 1 MarDiv Guerrilla Hunt

Under General Ridgway's leadership, the EUSA managed to bring the CCF's so-called third phase offensive to a halt in early January 1951. The 1st Marine Division received the assignment to clear an area encompassing about 40 square miles, as seen on this map of a stranded NKPA division in what became known as 'the Pohang Guerrilla Hunt'. (USMC)

Two Marines stand guard over a captured North Korean soldier while a US Navy corpsman administers first-aid to the prisoners. The stranded NKPA division stuck behind the ROKA lines was estimated to consist of around 6,000 soldiers with no heavy weapons. The enemy division had dispersed into smaller bands to conduct raids on UN communication and supply lines. (*USMC*)

It took the 1st Marine Division until mid-February 1951 to clear their assigned area of the threat posed by the NKPA soldiers. For the Marine officers, it proved a great training exercise to get their new replacements into shape and ready for more serious fighting. A Marine M26 Pershing medium tank, identified by its double-baffle muzzle brake, is shown taking part in the Pohang Guerrilla Hunt. (*USMC*)

(**Opposite, above**) In the summer of 1951, the 1st Marine Division received its first M46 Patton medium tanks. Rather than a new tank, it was a modernized M26 Pershing medium tank. An external spotting feature was the engine exhaust that was ejected through a top centre grill out of pipes extending sideways to large covered mufflers mounted on the rear of each tank's fenders, as seen in this picture. (*USMC*)

(**Opposite, below**) A 1951 US Army report listed unconfirmed sightings of Soviet Army heavy tanks, including the IS-3, in CFF service. In 1951 the CCF received the T-34-85 medium tank and units of the IS-2M, pictured here, from the Soviet Union. One reference source explains that there is photographic evidence of CCF IS-2M heavy tanks in North Korea. However, there is no American record of these appearing in combat. (*Pierre-Olivier Buan*)

(**Above**) In mid-January 1951, with the latest CCF offensive having ground to a halt, General Ridgway, the new commander of the EUSA, ordered a series of limited offensives. For the first three, only Marine air power took part. The 1st Marine Division would play a key part in the last four, following the Pohang Guerrilla Hunt. Pictured here are Marines heading for central Korea to stop another CCF offensive labelled the 'fourth phase'. (*USMC*)

(**Above**) A Marine appears in this image during the start of Operation KILLER, fourth in the series of seven limited offensives against the CCF in central Korea. KILLER was followed by Operations RIPPER, RUGGED and DAUNTLESS, the last concluded on 12 April. Some proved more successful than others, but they did achieve the goal of pushing UN forces 20 miles past the 38th Parallel. (*USMC*)

(**Opposite, above**) An F4U-4 Corsair is shown seconds before taking off from a US Navy aircraft carrier. Operation RIPPER, the fifth of seven limited offensives against the CCF in central Korea which included the 1st Marine Division, lasted from 7 March until 4 April. The goal of RIPPER and the other six limited offensives ordered by Ridgway was to inflict maximum punishment on the enemy and keep them off-balance. (*USMC*)

(**Opposite, below**) General Ridgway had seen what happened to the EUSA under its previous commander with UN forces tied to the roads, and outflanked repeatedly by the NKPA and CCF using the hills on either side of the roads. For his series of seven limited offensives, Ridgway insisted on his troops taking the high ground before advancing. Pictured here are Marines trudging up yet another steep Korean hill. (*USMC*)

(**Opposite, above**) Besides 105mm and 155mm howitzers, the 11th Marine (Artillery) Regiment had a single battery of T66 Rocket-Launchers, as pictured here, during the Korean War. The towed launcher had twenty-four tubes arrayed in three rows of eight. Deployed in April 1945, it arrived in Marine Corps' service to see combat during the Second World War. (*USMC*)

(**Opposite, below**) The Marine Corps' T66 fired the M16 4.5in 110mm spin-stabilized unguided rocket that was 31in in length, weighed 42.5lb and could strike targets out to a maximum range of 5,200 yards (3.1 miles). One of the problems when using the T66 that is obvious in this Korean War photograph is the visual signature that left it highly vulnerable to enemy counter-battery fire. (*USMC*)

(**Above**) Showing up in Marine Corps' service in 1951 was the HRS-1 pictured here, designed and built by Sikorsky. Much larger than earlier helicopters in service with the corps, it had a cargo compartment that, in theory, could carry eight passengers besides its two pilots. Top speed was 80 mph. Those in US Army and USAF service received the designation H-19. (*USMC*)

(**Above**) The Marines would make productive use of the HRS-1 during the Korean War, as is portrayed in this artist's impression of the helicopter. Despite that, the HRS-1 proved underpowered and had reliability issues that resulted in their grounding on several occasions during the conflict. None were shot down by enemy action, but a number crashed while hovering and two went down due to in-flight engine failures. (*USMC*)

(**Opposite, above**) A new aircraft in the Marine Corps' inventory that appeared during the Korean War in 1951 was the AD-2 Skyraider pictured here. The 1st MAW would eventually put into service two squadrons of the aircraft operating from land bases. It was very popular with Marine ground units due to its great ordnance-carrying capability. A total of 128 Marine Corps and US Navy Skyraiders went down during the Korean conflict, 101 of which were destroyed by enemy action. (*USMC*)

(**Opposite, below**) The AN/MPQ-14 was a ground-directing radar seen here in use during the Korean War by the Marine Corps. Developed between 1946 and 1950, it provided release-point information to Marine night-fighting Corsairs to put ordnance on the unseen enemy below them. It had an operational range of approximately 20,000 yards (11 miles). (*USMC*)

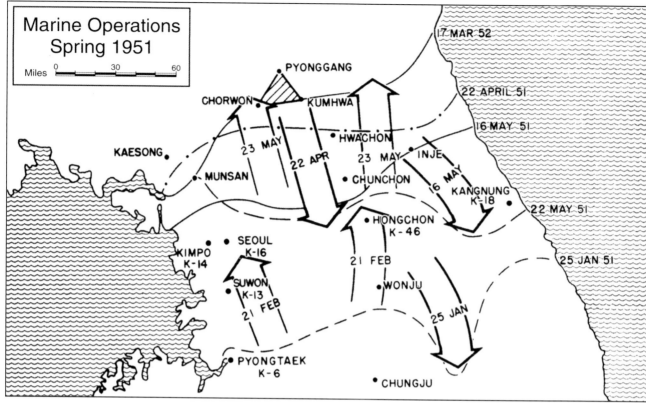

Marine Operations Spring 1951

Miles 0 30 60

PYONGGANG

17 MAR 52

CHORWON KUMHWA

22 APRIL 51

16 MAY 51

HWACHON

KAESONG

23 MAY

22 APR

23 MAY INJE

16 MAY

MUNSAN

CHUNCHON

KANGNUNG K-18

22 MAY 51

HONGCHON K-46

SEOUL K-16

KIMPO K-14

21 FEB

25 JAN 51

SUWON K-13

WONJU

21 FEB

25 JAN

PYONGTAEK K-6

CHUNGJU

(**Above**) The back and forth attacks and counterattacks by the 1st Marine Division, and by default the EUSA, in the spring of 1951 appear on this map. General Ridgway could not stop the CCF and the reconstituted NKPA forces from mounting new large-scale offensive operations, but once they ran their course, he would immediately counter-attack to keep the enemy off-balance with no time to reorganize. (*USMC*)

(**Right**) On 11 April 1951, American President Harry S. Truman relieved MacArthur from his various command positions due to the latter's continued efforts to widen the scope of the war, including the bombing of Red China and the proposed use of nuclear weapons. Ridgway, pictured here, the EUSA commander, was promoted to four-star general and named as MacArthur's successor. (*US Army*)

(**Opposite, above**) A Marine Corps' 81mm mortar team in action during the Korean War. By the beginning of June 1951, the EUSA, including the 1st Marine Division, were approximately back where they had been in April 1951 when the first step in the enemy's fifth phase had pushed them back across the 38th Parallel. That enemy offensive halted on 20 May 1951. (*USMC*)

(**Opposite, below**) A Marine carefully inspects an enemy defensive position for any signs of occupancy. From a 1951 US Army report is this extract describing NKPA defensive practices: 'Dummy positions and emplacements and false defenses are allegedly constructed whenever time permits in order to mislead UN air and ground reconnaissance and attacking forces.' (*USMC*)

184

A Marine photographer captures the moment that an unoccupied enemy bunker is destroyed to prevent its re-use. Both the CCF and the NKPA often built tunnels in which were emplaced everything from anti-tank guns to artillery pieces. A US Army manual on field fortifications mentions that tunnels require two entrances for ventilation. (*USMC*)

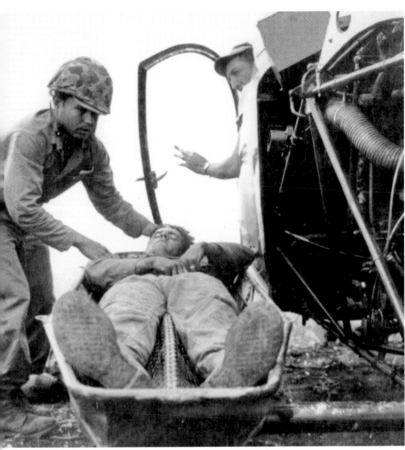

A wounded Marine appears on one of the two external stretchers pods on an HTL helicopter. A serious issue with the HTL-4 was that it lacked adequate instrumentation or backlighting of the existing instruments. On the positive side, the helicopter could fly the badly-wounded to hospital ships when seas were too rough for boats. (*USMC*)

In Korea, we see a water-cooled .30 calibre Browning M1917A1 heavy machine gun firing upon the enemy. To help keep Marine machine guns supplied with ammunition, as well as other weapons in an infantry unit, the 1st Marine Division had almost 300 Korean labourers to assist in construction and bring supplies to front-line positions; these were nicknamed 'Chiggy Bearers' or porters. (*USMC*)

(**Above**) The Marine Corps' replacement for the prop-driven F7F Tigercat in the all-weather night-fighting role in late 1952 was the twin-engine F3D-2 Skyknight jet fighter pictured here. Radar-equipped, the aircraft was armed with four 20mm automatic cannon and had a top speed of 565 mph and a cruising speed of 340 mph. Range was about 1,500 miles. (*USMC*)

(**Opposite, above**) Pictured here is the Marine Corps' F2H-2P photo reconnaissance version of the F2H-2 Banshee jet fighter that appeared in the Korean War in 1952. The same variant of the Banshee series also served with the US Navy during the conflict. The aircraft had six cameras, three on either side of its enlarged nose section that could be moved by the pilot from within his aircraft. (*USMC*)

(**Opposite, below**) In 1952, the Marine Corps placed into service a modified version of its F4U-4 Corsair series optimized for the low-level ground-attack role seen here and designated the AU-1. It featured extra armour around the pilot's cockpit and the aircraft's fuel tanks. The aircraft's oil coolers were relocated inboard to reduce vulnerability to ground fire. Fully loaded, the AU-1 weighed 20 per cent more than the standard Corsair. (*USMC*)

(**Above**) Marine Corps engineers are shown trying to disarm an enemy mine in Korea. From a 1949 US Army manual on mine warfare appears this extract on anti-tank mines: 'The fuze is usually the pressure type, either percussion or chemical. Although the impact of a running man may set them off, anti-tank mines usually are not dangerous to personnel.' (*USMC*)

(**Opposite, above**) By the summer of 1951, peace talks had begun. When ongoing, the fighting generally came to a stop and resumed when they halted. In November 1951 large-scale offensive operations were suspended for a month in November 1951 by the EUSA and indefinitely the following month. The intensity of the fighting grew in the spring of 1952. From a US Army manual is this illustration of a defensive position. (*US Army*)

(**Opposite, below**) Marine replacements are seen arriving in Korea. With large-scale offensive operations no longer possible as of November 1951 the fighting between both sides revolved around constant patrolling by both sides and raids on each other's defensive positions for prisoners. At the same time both sides began winterizing their fortifications. (*USMC*)

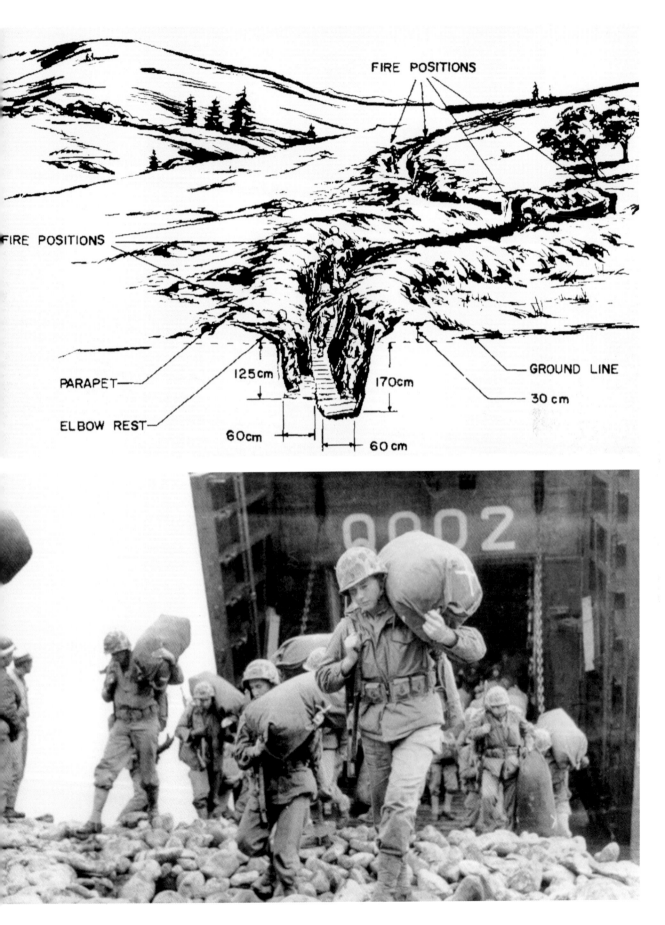

FIRE POSITIONS

FIRE POSITIONS

PARAPET

ELBOW REST

125 cm

60 cm

170 cm

60 cm

GROUND LINE

30 cm

Chapter Five

The Fighting Goes On

From the beginning of the Korean War through to the summer of 1952, the CCF and NKPA made little use of artillery. According to a US Army report dated September 1951, the artillery employed by the enemy was considered 'obsolete, or worn out and in constant need of maintenance'. The report did note, however, that captured enemy officers stated they would be receiving substantial aid in the form of artillery and other weapons from the Soviet Union.

With Soviet military aid, the number of artillery pieces in the CCF and NKPA inventory grew in number during the winter of 1952/53. At the same time, the effectiveness of the enemy artillery grew. In a USMC historical publication there appears an extract describing the CCF use of artillery during fighting in October 1952:

> Calculations of total incoming ran from 15,500 to 34,000 rounds during the 36-hour engagement … In any event, the 12,500 rounds the 7th Marine [Regiment] received during the first 24 hours represented the heaviest bombardment any Marine regiment had been subjected to up to that time. Moreover, it had now become clearly evident that the enemy could stockpile a plentiful supply of ammunition, despite attempts of UN aircraft to interfere with the enemy's flow of supplies.

In the Trenches

It would take another Korean winter before the tempo of fighting between the Marines of the 1st Division and the CCF decreased along the Jamestown Line. As the Korean winter continued into the early months of 1953, static warfare conditions prevailed with success by either side measured in yards, not miles. Life for the lower-ranking combatants revolved around their trench lines and the wood and sandbag bunkers in which they slept. The Marines nicknamed their bunkers 'sandbag castles'.

Some of the Marine bunkers were configured as fighting positions, as they had firing ports for machine guns and accommodation for their crews. Other bunkers served as living quarters for anywhere from five to ten Marines. Outside each bunker used as living quarters were fighting holes for the Marines that resided within. One

Marine described the fighting holes as 'simply a niche in the forward wall of the trench, usually covered with planks and a few sandbags.'

Typically, each Marine fighting hole had an earthen shelf for a few hand grenades and a sound-powered telephone linking him to the company command post. Added protection for the Marines manning a trench came from indentations dug into the trench wall nicknamed 'rabbit holes'. They provided a degree of overhead protection from enemy artillery and mortar barrages.

During the Korean winter, the Marines' watches in their fighting holes were often limited to forty-five minutes before returning to the warmth of their bunker. Most of the bunkers intended as living quarters had kerosene or oil stoves, vented through the roof, to provide heat. Within the bunkers close to the main line candles provided light, while those further to the rear had electric lights powered by gasoline generators.

A Marine corporal recounted in a USMC historical publication a description of the Jamestown Line at the beginning of 1953 as 'A messy, rambling series of ditches 5 to 7 feet deep' with the bunkers themselves surrounded by 'piles of trash, ration cans, scrap paper, and protruding stove pipes' revealing their location to the enemy. The always-present trash also led to the disgusting presence of rats, nicknamed 'bunker bunnies' by Marines.

In spite of the fact that the bunkers delivered much-needed protection from the elements, the junior officers of the 1st Marine Division actually considered the bunkers to be a problem, as the comfort they afforded sapped the combat drive of the enlisted ranks and provided a large target to the enemy if they penetrated Marine defensive lines.

Armour

In February 1953, the Marines of the 1st Division launched two raids on CCF lines to destroy enemy defensive positions. Besides close-support aircraft and artillery, Marine tanks, including flame-thrower tanks, did their part to suppress the enemy as the raids progressed. From a USMC historical publication is a description of some of the fighting engaged in by Marine flame-thrower tanks:

> On the ground, flame was found to be the best weapon for neutralizing the well-fortified CCF caves. From Company A, 1st Tank Battalion came information about Chinese 3.5-inch rocket launcher teams used in antitank defense. Several of these tank-killer teams had run down the trench-line holding small bushes in front of them. The enemy then boldly advanced through a hail of bullets to within 15–20 yards of the Marine tank before opening fire with their rockets. Short bursts of flame from headquarters tanks soon caused even the most intrepid to beat a hurried retreat.

Air Power

Much to the delight of the 1st Marine Division, by the beginning of 1953 the Fifth Air Force had switched their primary focus from the air superiority and interdiction roles to the close-support role. Due to the danger of Fifth Air Force aircraft attacking friendly troops by mistake, only those enemy targets a minimum of 3,000 yards or more in front of EUSA positions received authorization for an attack. For the Marine pilots of the 1st MAW, this was a dramatic change as the year before they would drop ordnance within 100 yards of friendly positions.

A description of one type of close-support mission flown by 1st MAW pilots appears in a passage from a USMC historical publication:

> Close air support missions were of two types. The first and used the most, appeared in the frag [an abbreviated form of an operation order] as an assignment of a certain number of aircraft to report to a specific control point at a specific time, for use by that unit as required or specified. Applicable intelligence and coordinating information would be included most of the time, and ordnance would either be specified or assigned as a standard load. Depending on the target, if one was specified in the frag, flights of this type were usually of four aircraft but could often be as many as eight or twelve.

Back into Reserve

In February 1953, US Army Lieutenant General Maxwell Taylor assumed command of the EUSA from Lieutenant General Van Fleet. One of his first actions was to put the 1st Marine Division in the EUSA reserve as it had been in the front line since August 1951. He felt that the Marine division required eight weeks of refresher training to bring it back to maximum effectiveness.

To replace the 1st Marine Division, the new EUSA commander brought in the US Army 25th Infantry Division, along with an attached Turkish brigade. The changeover was to be completed by 5 May. There was, however, a catch. The 11th Marine (Artillery) Regiment and the Marine 1st Tank Battalion were to remain behind in support of the 25th Infantry Division.

The Marine tanks went into semi-fixed positions along the main line of resistance (MLR). To re-supply the tanks the US Army attached M39 Armored Utility Vehicles to the two Marine tank companies. A significant advantage of having the tanks in position along the MLR came from their onboard radios, as they provided an alternative means of communication when enemy artillery fire severed phone wires.

Again and Again

On 25 May 1953, the CCF launched a series of major attacks on the Turkish brigade attached to the 25th Infantry Division. Eventually, a total of thirty-three Marine tanks were engaged in trying to repulse the enemy assault on the UN soldiers. By 28 May an entire CCF division attempted to overrun the Turkish brigade. However, with the Marine tanks and UN artillery firing 9,800 rounds, the enemy attack crumbled.

In the meantime, the EUSA commander ordered the 1st Marine Division then in reserve to prepare for a counterattack if the enemy broke through Turkish lines. Heavy rains on 30 May that turned everything to mud dashed any hope the enemy had of continuing their assault. As a truce agreement between the warring sides was on the verge of acceptance at the end of May 1953, the EUSA commander decided not to counterattack the enemy with the 1st Marine Division.

The CCF would not relent, even as the details of a truce agreement were agreed upon by both sides. Between 10 and 16 June they launched a series of fierce assaults on the ROKA II Corps. They managed to push it back 4,000 yards to new defensive positions, which proved a far cry from the CCF attacks in April and May 1951. These attacks penetrated ROKA defensive lines along many miles. The ROKA had improved over time and had become a more battle-hardened force by 1953.

It took until 18 June for the ROKA II Corps to turn back the CCF. The CCF, however, had not finished, and between 6 and 10 July they launched an even larger assault on the ROKA II Corps, causing them to lose two critical defensive positions. To assist the hard-pressed ROKA divisions, the 1st MAW entered the fray. The 7th Marine Infantry Regiment was also alerted for a possible counterattack in case the CCF broke through ROKA lines. However, that did not happen and the enemy's attacks ceased by the end of the month.

Once More

On 7 July the 1st Marine Division replaced the 25th Infantry Division and its attached Turkish brigade along the former Jamestown Line. The EUSA commander had ordered that the use of various names to identify sections of the MLR be discontinued as of 28 April. From that day on, UN defensive lines became simply the MLR.

The enemy mounted an ever-increasing number of probing infantry patrols and artillery barrages to greet the returning Marines on 7 and 8 July. These activities continued until the CCF launched larger attacks on the nights of 19 and 20 July against the most forward Marine outposts, which did fall. Both sides then engaged in an endless series of artillery barrages.

An End to the Fighting

As a possible ceasefire seemed to be only days away, on the morning of 20 July, a half-hour before the Marines of the 1st Division were to counterattack, a message came from the EUSA commander:

> The outposts in front of the MLR had gradually lost their value in my opinion because, between the MLR and the outposts, minefields, tactical wire, etc. had

made their reinforcement and counterattacks very costly ... and holding poor real estate for sentimental reasons is a poor excuse for undue casualties.

On the evening of 27 July 1953 an armistice came into effect, bringing a halt to more than three long years of fighting in Korea. The opponents all pulled back from their existing MLRs, and all their hard-fought former fighting positions sat abandoned.

A 4,000-yard-wide no man's land that crossed the Korean Peninsula from west to east and was labelled the Demilitarized Zone (DMZ) was set up. It was located just above the 38th Parallel where the conflict had begun on 25 June 1950 when the NKPA crossed into South Korea.

The 1st Marine Division would continue to staff new defensive positions established south of the new DMZ until mid-March 1955. At that point, it turned over its positions to the US Army 24th Infantry Division. The Marines of the 1st Division arrived at their home base at Camp Pendleton in April 1955.

Summing Up

Total American military casualties for the Korean War came in at approximately 140,000 men. These included about 25,000 killed and around 100,000 wounded, with another 13,000 missing presumed dead. Out of those numbers, the Marines lost 4,267 dead and 26,034 wounded. The total numbers of dead include killed in action, died of wounds, captured and died, missing in action and presumed dead. The 1st MAW lost a total of 436 aircraft which included those in operational accidents.

A total of forty-two Medals of Honor were awarded to the men of the 1st Marine Division during the Korean War and five attached US Navy corpsmen. The division itself received three US Presidential Unit Citations, as well as a US Navy unit commendation.

Leadership of the 1st Marine Division during the Korean War would pass through several hands. Major General Oliver P. Smith turned over the division to Major General Gerald C. Thomas in April 1951. He, in turn, passed it on to Major General John T. Selden, seen on the left of the photograph. Command of the division then went to Major General Edwin A. Pollock shown on the right of the image in August 1952. *(USMC)*

(**Above**) During the winter of 1952 into 1953, Marine tanks (and US Army tanks) often found themselves assigned to the role of mobile pillboxes to bolster the defences of hard-pressed infantry units. In this photograph we see two Marine M46 Patton medium tanks on the crest of a hill. In this role they spent most of their time engaged in 'bunker-busting'. (*USMC*)

(**Opposite, above**) The problem with employing tanks in the bunker-busting role is that many main gun rounds are required to confirm destruction, leading to premature wearing-out of the tank main gun barrel, and the difficulty of replacing them in the front lines. A Marine Corps' M46 Patton tank vehicle commander and loader observe the local Korean terrain. (*USMC*)

(**Opposite, below**) With the advent of static warfare in Korea beginning in late 1951, the Soviet Union began supplying the NKPA and the CCF with a large number of heavier artillery pieces ranging from 122mm up to 152mm. In this museum picture, we see a Second World War-era 122mm howitzer M1931/37 (A-19). The weapon had a range of approximately 12 miles. (*Vladimir Yakubov*)

(**Opposite, above**) To supplement its medium tanks' fire-power in the defensive role going into 1952 and 1953, the Marine Corps brought forward some of its LVT(A)-4 amphibious tractors as seen in this image. The example shown had the post-war-added roof armour. Thinly-armoured with tracks that had a very short off-road service life, it was far from the perfect choice for the role. (*USMC*)

(**Opposite, below**) Note a large number of hand grenades present in this Marine Corps' position. When attacked at night, defenders found grenades typically proved more effective than small arms at short ranges. The Marines employed the standard Fragmentation Hand Grenade Mk II. The manual says: 'you release the grenade with a snapping motion of the wrist just before your arm is fully extended and let it roll off the tips of your fingers.' (*USMC*)

(**Above**) In this photograph we see the results of Marines policing up a local battlefield by collecting enemy dead for quick burial; a no doubt most disagreeable job. In spite of the heavy reliance the Marines placed on their artillery support, there were times when transportation breakdowns led to ammunition shortages. Making matters even worse was that the NKPA artillery at times outnumbered those in the 1st Marine Division inventory. (*USMC*)

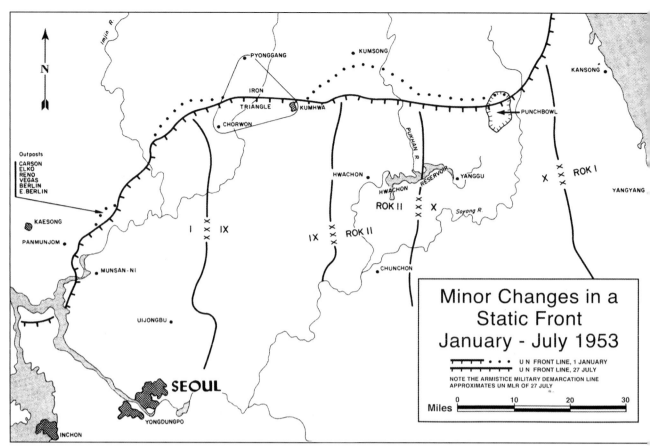

Minor Changes in a
Static Front
January - July 1953

UN FRONT LINE, 1 JANUARY
UN FRONT LINE, 27 JULY

NOTE THE ARMISTICE MILITARY DEMARCATION LINE
APPROXIMATES UN MLR OF 27 JULY

Miles

(**Opposite, above**) With this map it is possible to see how, during the first half of 1953, the fighting was restricted to a very limited area and was very akin to the trench warfare stalemate of the First World War. The area marked as 'the Punchbowl' was an ancient volcanic crater captured by the 1st Marine Division in September 1951, allowing the UN forces to hold it till the end of the war. (*USMC*)

(**Opposite, below**) An interesting picture of a Marine in Korea operating a Browning .50 calibre M2 air-cooled machine gun fitted with a sniper scope. From a Marine Corps historical publication appears the following passage: 'More heirs of the Japanese military than the Soviets, the North Koreans showed no hesitation in launching counterattacks large and small and from unexpected directions.' (*USMC*)

(**Above**) Pictured here is a Marine 75mm recoilless rifle crew in action. All are wearing the M1951 armoured vest, delivery of which to the 1st Marine Division was completed by November 1952, including 400 sets of lower torso armour. The armoured vest weighed 7.75lb and was a zippered sleeveless jacket constructed of water-resistant nylon containing two types of armour: a nylon weave and another referred to as Doron. (*USMC*)

(**Above**) To assist the Marine Corps in defending its hilltop defensive positions, the US Army provided some M39 Armored Utility Vehicles. These open-topped vehicles, based on the chassis of the Second World War M18 Tank Destroyers, saw use in a variety of roles. This included ammunition re-supply – as seen in this picture – casualty evacuation, and improvised troop transports. (*USMC*)

(**Opposite, above**) Late in the Korean War the NKPA and the CCF acquired a supply of 75mm recoilless rifles and a large number of captured American 3.5in rocket-launchers that posed a serious threat to both Marine Corps and US Army tanks. In this photograph we see Marines erecting a heavy wire screen around the turret of an M46 Patton medium tank to detonate shaped-charge warheads. (*USMC*)

(**Opposite, below**) Among the heavy artillery pieces supplied to the NKPA and the CCF late in the Korean War was the 152mm Howitzer M1943 (D-1) seen in this museum photograph. With a muzzle brake, the weapon fired an 88lb high-explosive (HE) round out to a maximum range of around 12,320 yards (7 miles). Reflecting the weight and size of the rounds, the rate of fire came out to no more than three to four per minute. (*Vladimir Yakubov*)

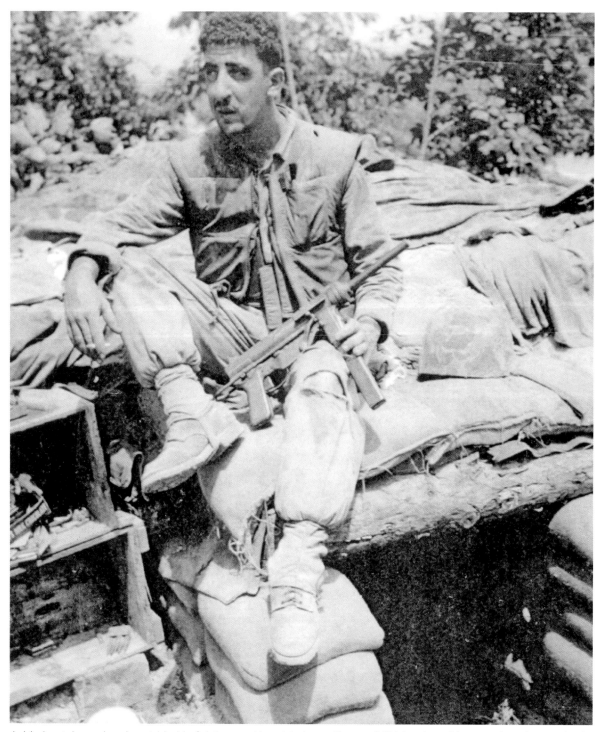

A Marine takes a break outside his fighting position. He is cradling an M3A1 submachine gun best known by its nickname of the 'Grease Gun'. A total of 15,000 were manufactured before the end of the Second World War with another 33,000 made post-war. It was the replacement for the M1 submachine gun best known as the 'Thompson', which also appeared in Korean War service with the Marine Corps. (*USMC*)

A 1st Marine Division defensive trench with everyone wearing armoured vests. In no way bulletproof, the armoured vest still quickly proved its worth by dramatically reducing the number of killed and wounded. Its downside was that it became very uncomfortable very quickly due to heat build-up and, of course, added weight. The US Army adopted a slightly different version of an armoured vest. *(USMC)*

(**Above**) The replacement for the H03S-1 helicopter in Marine Corps' service was the H05S, also designed and built by Sikorsky. The first units appeared in service in January 1952. It was the first American military helicopter with all-metal blades. In the medical casualty evacuation role, stretcher patients were loaded through the front of the cockpit as pictured here. (*USMC*)

(**Opposite, above**) In the last year of the war, the Marine Corps experimented with white light searchlights mounted on the gun shield of their M46 Patton medium tanks. As their use tended to attract a great deal of enemy return fire, the Marine Corps went on to experiment with infrared searchlights, as seen in this photograph. The programme received the name 'Leaflet II'. (*USMC*)

(**Opposite, below**) Belonging to the 1st MAW was the 1st 90mm AAA Gun Battalion seen here guarding Pusan. The weapon fired a 23.4lb high-explosive (HE) round with the projectile leaving the barrel at 2,700ft per second. The maximum ceiling for the gun was 39,500ft. The combination of gun and mount together weighed in at 32,000lb and required a 6 × 6 truck for towing. (*USMC*)

(**Right**) Posing on his USAF F-86 fighter jet during the Korean War is exchange Marine pilot Major John F. Bolt. On 12 July 1953, he shot down his sixth enemy MiG-15 jet fighter, becoming the Marine Corps' first jet ace. He had also achieved ace status during the Second World War by shooting down six Japanese aircraft while flying with the well-known Black Sheep squadron VMF-214; the only person to become an ace in both wars. (*USMC*)

(**Opposite, above**) A future astronaut and later United States senator, Marine Corps Major John H. Glenn poses in the cockpit of a USAF F-86 fighter jet. During his time in the Korean War Glenn shot down three enemy MiG-15 jet fighters as an exchange pilot with the USAF. Famous American baseball players Ted Williams and Gerald F. 'Jerry' Coleman also flew missions during the Korean War; the former in the Panther and the latter in the Corsair. (*USMC*)

(**Opposite, below**) Peace talks (armistice talks) began on 8 July 1951 at a South Korean city known as Kaesong, south of the 38th Parallel and about 35 miles north-east of the South Korean capital of Seoul. On 25 July 1951, the peace talks moved to the site pictured here near the North Korean village of Panmunjom. The area then became a demilitarized island surrounded by fighting but linked to South Korea by a single road for access by the peace negotiators. (*USMC*)

(**Opposite, above**) There was a ceasefire agreement (truce) by the warring factions on 27 July 1953 in which both sides withdrew from their most forward position by 2,000 yards, creating a 4,000-yard Demilitarized Zone (DMZ) between them. The 1st Marine Division provided a 1,000-man detachment to police their side of the DMZ. Pictured here is an M4A3 with a dummy main gun configured as a command and control vehicle. (*USMC*)

(**Opposite, below**) North Korean officers are seen here with their American counterparts at Panmunjom, fine-tuning the armistice. Despite the truce and the establishment of the DMZ, the 1st Marine Division remained extremely vigilant in case fighting started once again. To save on manpower, the Marines set up a large number of automatic weapons along their new defensive positions on the southern side of the DMZ. (*USMC*)

(**Above**) Pictured here is a Marine MP assigned as part of the 1,000-man detachment to police the newly-created DMZ. These MPs acted as armed escorts on the road to Panmunjom, carrying rifles and pistols. They also staffed many fixed observation posts and conducted roving patrols to report any unusual activities within the DMZ. (*USMC*)

The 1st Division Marines remained in South Korea along the DMZ until March 1955 when they turned over that job to a US Army division. Pictured here are Marines climbing aboard US Navy attack transports for the much-anticipated trip back home. The 1st MAW would not depart South Korea until June 1956. (*USMC*)

Notes

Notes

Notes

Notes

Notes

Notes

Notes

Notes

Notes

Notes